The Wretched of the Earth and —Me

The Wretched of the Earth and —Me

by

Minerva Davis

This edition digitally re-mastered and
published by JM Classic Editions © 2009
Original text © Minerva Davis 1992

ISBN 978-1-906600-11-2

All rights reserved. No part of this book subject
to copyright may be reproduced in any form or
by any means without prior permission in writing
from the publisher.

For Adriane, Louise and Nicholas.

Contents

List of Illustrations	ix
Prologue	xi
Got vit helfen	1
Our *shiftscarten*	10
The Hebrew Immigrant Aid Society	13
Dora and Giogiu	17
Dora's Toronto	26
Mrs Henry Shilling	33
My Toronto	39
Sweet Marie or *Turkish Delight*?	47
The Study Circle	58
Life *a la* Jimmy Higgins	72
Emma Goldman in Toronto	83
I get to go to University	91
Signs and Portents	98
Rebel Girl	102
Fools Rush In	110
Isms or the Impure in Thought	124
General Draper's iron heel	130
Jobless again	137
Minnie in Manitoba	144
Deeply Underground	157
On the Banks of the French River	161
Goat Mountain	165
The Worker	170
Death in Karelia	176
Back in the Mainstream	180

List of Illustrations

Falticheni c. 1919	2
Bucharest c. 1919	2
Naples c. 1919	6
Rome c. 1919	7
Paris c. 1919	8
Ellis Isle c. 1919	12
Toronto c. 1919	15
Dora c. 1919	18
Dancing the *Hora*	20
Hanlan's Point, Toronto, c. 1910	28
High Park, Toronto, c. 1910	28
The CNE, c. 1910	29
The Comique Theatre, Toronto, c. 1910	29
The Red Army, c. 1917	37
Factory, King St., Toronto c. 1919	41
Harbord St. Collegiate, Toronto, c. 1920	45
Coal & wood-burning stove, c. 1920	49
Girl's outfit, Toronto, c. 1920	50
Ladies' outfit, c. 1920	53
Richmond St. Toronto, c. 1925	57
Shea's, Toronto, c. 1925	60
Eaton's, Toronto, c. 1925	63
Royal Ontario Museum, Toronto, c. 1925	64
Victor Himmelfarb, c. 1920	65
Charley Marriot, c. 1919	67
Marie Tiboldo, c. 1930	84
Emma Goldman, c. 1930	85
Flatbush Ave., Brooklyn, NY c. 1927	92
Harlem, NY, c. 1927	95
The author c. 1929	101
Jack MacDonald c. 1929	111
Maurice Spector c. 1929	112

The Communist Eight 1931   156
Clara & David White, c. 1930   169
Aate Pitkanen & father c. 1930   176

PROLOGUE

"Where do they go after 4 o'clock?" I asked about the unemployed who filled the former church in the dread winter of 1931 in downtown Winnipeg,

"To the 'jungle,' Minnie, to the 'jungle' on the banks of the Red River. Yeh, it's cold. But they make fires...Sometimes the police stage raids, handcuff the men while they're sleeping and drag them off to jail. The foreign-born ones are deported."

In 1992, Communism, hitherto influencing half of the world, is adjudged by its own as a fatally flawed system, perhaps an unspeakably tragic mistake.

Whether reform of this system is possible, whether shreds of the Marxist ideal of "from each according to his ability to each according to his needs" can be incorporated in the social pattern of the times to come is for the future to tell.

But what was its attraction for more than one hundred years for the dispossessed, for the disadvantaged, for those who felt the yoke of exploitation? What did it promise?

In my lifetime I found it was not the promises that beckoned as much as the misery, despair and hopelessness of an unrestrained capitalism that pushed the wretched of the earth to struggle for a better society. They apparently saw the ideal in the Communist system. Its flaws were forgiven, for once you committed yourself to communism, you made an irrevocable choice. There was no road back.

We left Roumania in 1919. I was twelve years of age. My father had the only tavern in Rasca, the little mill town where I was born. The peasants came on Sundays to dance *the hora*. In the woods the cuckoo sang in the springtime and the workers had their little plot of land and their chickens.

For our family, too, life was good.

Every now and then men came down from the mountain areas bringing brook trout in beds of woven pine. In the spring, a young lamb was bought and slaughtered by the shochet, who was empowered to butcher according to Jewish ritual. Sometimes there would be goose which father smoked by simply climbing up on the roof and hanging it down the chimney flue.

But not everyone was satisfied.

Out of sheer boredom and frustration, sister Dora committed an unspeakable 'scandale' that initiated our immigration to 'America.' Dora was the first to be sent away, followed by sisters Rosie and Molly .

In 1919, with the remaining two young girls in tow, Mama, illiterate and unsophisticated, with little money but with "Got vit helfen" on her lips, leads on, through a disorganized Europe in a fantastically roundabout way which included Rome and Paris to New York, where the odyssey ends by the trio being ordered to be deported whence they came.

Rescued by an angel from the Hebrew Immigrant Aid Society, (H.I.A.S.) we arrive in Toronto in June 1919, to be plunged immediately into the factory system. My dream, from the age of 10 on, was to go to University.

What was I doing then at age 12 in a paper box factory?

In 1919, The Compulsory School Attendance Act called for all children to attend school to age 16. However, a child was allowed to work at 14 under a special permit. Consequently, most working-class children went to work at 14.

My 'room and board' was a very welcome contribution to a family's budget when wages of a major bread-winner was not more than $18 a week. My first pay was $7 and I paid $5 room and board.

A paper box factory, a chocolate factory, a printing firm had to deal with my unenthusiastic and reluctant help until sister Molly paved the way to my attending school—but not for long.

The way to university was very arduous and without end. (I never got there.) I escaped the factory system by taking a night-school course, becoming a stenographer and then a self-taught bookkeeper.

But I could not escape the humiliation of being a 'greeny.' Even after I achieved fluency in English, I still had the tell-tale accent of a newcomer. In the '20s, a foreign accent was a key to rejection and disdain. I ached to be accepted, to be as Canadian as Orangemen and women who paraded so magnificently on my birthday.

Joining the Young Communist League at 18 years of age brought me into a new world, a world of acceptance, of realization of self worth, a chance to work for an ideal of a better world for oneself and for others. A new world was in birth and I ingested it all with joy.

Communism built its own world, its own philosophy, its own social structure, comradeship, and security of a non-economic sort. It erected a closed system from which it was very difficult to break out.

Even after the 20th Congress of the Communist Party of the Soviet Union, which should have and perhaps did alert many to the crimes of Stalinism, when so many Party members were disillusioned, it was difficult for them to break away, not knowing what sort of a life they could have outside. (Nuns and priests encounter the same questioning and self doubt when considering leaving their hitherto secure psychological nests.)

I progressed up the ladder of Party work until I became a small-time functionary, and then found myself on a more important level as the wife of Charlie Marriott, who was Party organizer in Manitoba and then editor of *The Worker* for a time.

During the lean years from the formation of the Party (in the early '20s) and through the Depression, when the Party was at its best leading the struggles for relief, for unemployment insurance, for organizing the unorganized, money was always a problem and appointing full-time functionaries did not necessarily mean that they would have a living wage, or even enough to eat.

Eating, paying rent, was incidental to the work one had to do, to the struggle. There were functionaries who collected full-time salaries. This was in the range of $10 a week during the height of the Depression, and there were others who could not raise that and there was resentment.

The work of full-time functionaries was demanding, hard, never ending, largely unrewarding and subject to criticism from 'below' and from 'above.' Not only did they not have enough to eat, they had to be on the alert continually not to commit right or left deviations, not to advance reformist theories and, above all, to defend the Soviet Union on paper and by spoken word. Then there were real problems—with rent (we 'skipped' through the window at midnight sometimes), with babies who needed carriages and to be fed and with wives left at home with small children whose full-time functionary husbands could not send any money to feed the kids.

During the Depression people starved. There were no jobs. The young men were herded into work camps (an R.B. Bennett feature of government), where they were paid 25 cents a day. Relief was for families only and the rate varied. I myself was on relief at $2.25 a week, for a family of two adults and a child.

The Communist Party was active in organizing the unemployed to ask for bread, to fight deportation and all the indignities visited on them by a government which said: "I will not put a premium on idleness." (Prime Minister R.B. Bennett, 1930-1935)

I once met a French Canadian professor in Cuba who was vocal about being a Leninist.

"Oh," I said, "I was a Leninist once. I was a member of the Communist Party—during the Depression.

"Every intelligent person during the Depression had to be a member of the Communist Party," he said.

"And then, because of Stalin and sectarianism, I left the Party."

"That was the correct thing to do," he added. "Every era has its own requirements and Communism served a function when no one else offered leadership. Sure, the people turned away when Communism no longer represented their needs and aspirations and found its message hollow. But the work they had done was vital: they contributed no small part to the good society we have today."

Got vilt helfen

Letter in hand I run as fast as my chubby toddler legs can carry me. "Here, Mama! Rosie and Mali have sent us the money. We can now go to America!"

Nineteen nineteen, however, is not a very good year for emigrating to Canada from Roumania. Russia, a next door neighbor, is churning in the grip of an earth-shaking revolution. It is sending tremors far and near. and causing all of Europe to shudder like a disturbed jig saw puzzle. Every country is hugging its borders tightly, fearfully, and making travel safe is not the priority of any government. No regular schedule of ship or train exists, and commercial airlines are still in the realm of the fantastic future. Those who have to travel do so at their own peril.

Mama knows little of these matters, nothing of politics nor geography—a great advantage in her case. She does not read the one or two newspapers that sometimes reach our town, for she is practically illiterate, being able to read only a bit of her Hebrew prayer book. Actually, Mama learns to write on the road to America, allowing us to teach her to the point where she can, laboriously, write her name, thus becoming literate, a condition of entry into the New World.

Recently widowed, with two youngsters still to look after and left penniless by the ill fortunes of World War I, she knows only that the money sent by her daughters in America means salvation. What if her only travel experience has been a brief journey from the tiny village of Rasca to Falticeni, a distance of 20 kilometers? No matter! She tucks the money safely away perfectly certain that there is nothing to be afraid of, sure that "Got vilt helfen," (God will look after it.) She is intent only on the future of her two little girls, myself, Malica aged ten and Tutsica aged fifteen.

We begin our basic preparations at once. For three days Mama bakes continuously; bread for the immediate days ahead and a large quantity of *kichlach*, also called 'nothings,' a sort of sweet biscuit made without shortening which does not require expensive ingredients. Mama expects these biscuits to stay crisp and travel well.

The Wretched of the Earth—and Me

FaltichENI c. 1919

Bucharest c. 1919

Got vilt helfen

As an accompaniment, she makes a thick preserve out of green gage plums, which we pack in two large, gaily-decorated tea caddies. Being well sugared, this will last us a long time.

To my surprise and delight, we then go to a dressmaker for our travelling costumes, mine being a lightweight, raspberry-colored checked wool, complemented by a straw hat trimmed with a band of the same material. Mama orders a navy blue cheviot suit for herself and we are now ready for the journey.

Leaving the little sleepy town of Falticeni early on a day in June, we set out by train. A carpet of red poppies covering the fields to infinity cheerfully wave us on all the way to the capital, Bucharest.

Bucharest is the realized image of all my dreams of a big city.

From my acquaintance with French novels, I recognize the locale of many a story, for it has been built as a replica of Paris. I gaze, enchanted, at the wide boulevards, incredibly clean, and lined with trees. The beautiful buildings are ornamented with moulded cupids, angels and goddesses. Vast squares are adorned with innummerable flower beds, just bursting with heavenly color. Hansom cabs carry the elegant people of the capital around. There are even some automobiles to be seen. How rich everyone must be!

I was not far wrong for Bucharest was the cultural hub of the Balkans at this time, a stop on the Orient Express. And it was just the era of King Carol and Magda Lupescu—his beloved red-headed mistress, whom he married in exile on his death bed.

We have relatives here, my cousins, the Timen family, who are hospitable and kind. Best of all, they have children my age.

The next day, they are instructed to show their country cousins the sights. These include a famous monastery and a visit to La Cheoban, a very elegant salon, said to be frequented by members of the court. La Cheoban serves ice cream and French pastries. I am impressed with the cousins and especially happy with the pattiserie.

In the meantime, at home, the other cousins enthusiastically proceed to plan our voyage for us.

Vehement and wild sessions go on for days, during which every sentence starts with "Let them...."

"Let them go via Constantinopole. They could embark at Constanza and tour the Black Sea..."

"Let them go through the Dardanelles..."

The Wretched of the Earth—and Me

"Let them stop over in Greece and see the Acropolis..."
"Let them go to Naples, and see Vesuvius smoking..."
"Rome..."
"Paris..."

Enchanted with the sound of these romantic places, an elaborate tour is devised, which has more to do with our cousins unrealized dreams to travel Europe than with our necessity to take the shortest and cheapest route to America. Mama is too shy or embarrassed to tell these very sophisticated relatives that her daughters in Toronto, vague as everyone was as to our route, sent us very little money and that perhaps we could not afford to travel tourist to Naples.

There was no discussion on how much money we had nor how long we might be on the road, nor was it considered a problem that my mother spoke only Yiddish and Roumanian.

"My girls speak very good French, especially Malica," she volunteered We had a smattering in that language.

* * *

For that matter, I don't know how it came about that at age 10, I spoke "very good French." In retrospect, Roumania was practically a bilingual country—the other language being French. It inherited a largely Latin tongue from the Roman occupation when the country was known as Dacia. Napoleon III sent a member of his family to rule in Roumania, and the line held to King Michael who was deposed in 1947. Roumanians looked for their inspiration in culture and all things artistic to France, and sent their children to be educated in Paris, if they could afford it. To speak French was a sign of being sophisticated, educated, cultured. It was possible for children especially, to learn some French outside school. One picked it up from general conversation and from literature.

In fact, I do not even know how I learned to read and write at all, for in the last two years there had been no schooling in my life.

In 1914, after declaring war on the side of the Allies, the Roumanian government mysteriously closed all schools. My parents speculated that the buildings might be required for hospitals or barracks.

Month after month I patrolled the buildings and month after month I reported that there were no soldiers, wounded or otherwise, in the school.

"All government foolishness," said my father. "Who can ever understand it?"

Got vilt helfen

We knew a great deal about government foolishness in our family, my father having himself suffered previously from that governmental disease. When Roumania entered the war in 1914, the authorities in Falticeni, anxious to demonstrate their patriotism and vigilance, rounded up and arrested all the 'aliens' in the city. The 'aliens' they arrested were Jewish businessmen. As the Roumanian government had never bestowed citizenship on its Jewish population, there was a large pool of 'aliens' to choose from, most of whom had been in the country longer than any family could remember.

My father, however, was a citizen, a distinction bestowed on him as a result of having participated, as a soldier, in one of the many military quarrels Roumania had had with its neighbours.

Being a citizen enabled him to get a license to run a tavern and to sell tobacco. But no matter! He, too, was gathered in. After several days of incarceration the detainees were released one at the time, as the palms of officials, in good Roumanian gypsy style, were crossed with silver.

The closing of the school was a terrible blow to me for there was nothing for a child in the way of education or recreation. So my sister and I discovered books.

Tutsica concentrated on French novels but I didn't discriminate. I read every printed word I could find. I found books by Conan Doyle, Balzac, Alphonse Daudet, Victor Hugo—even Boccacio's *Decameron*. The books were paper-back editions, the new ones requiring their pages to be cut open with a knife.

There was no public library, of course, and these books were bought and passed around by Tutsica's friends. I had to learn to do some fast reading for Tutsica might decide to return a book before I was finished with it. She was very tolerant about my reading them but for a time she took to holding back. She read the books but kept them hidden while they were in her posession. Then I would run crying to Mama who would be very upset. There was so little she could give her youngest and she didn't want to see me cry.

"Let her read them," she said, "Give them to her."

"But Mama, she wouldn't understand these books. They are not suitable for her, Mama," protested Tutsica from her superior standpoint at fifteen years of age.

However I read them and what I didn't understand, I guessed at. The reading and the guessing constituted my education in Roumania. This

The Wretched of the Earth—and Me

education was a very lopsided but varied one, and thus it included my acquaintance with French words and phrases. Actually Tutsica and I could carry on a conversation in French, albeit a simple one.

* * *

Our cousins having completed planning our voyage, a large dried sausage is added to our provisions and we are now ready to set off for America.

The sea journey is really wasted on me. I can't see any difference between the Black Sea, the Bosphorus and the Aegian. It is all deep water, it always looks the same—either green or blue. On board ship the food, however, is more than satisfactory, especially the mountains of while bread and bowls of delicious marmalade. It is good to travel 'tourist class'—no crowds. Tutsica makes friends with a poet and his wife travelling to Italy for holidays.

We land in Naples and to my surprise there is Mount Vesuvius, 'smoking'—as promised by our cousins.

Naples c. 1919

Got vilt helfen

Rome, c. 1919

With no knowledge of Italian, without as much as a "*Got vilt helfen*," Mama hustles us out of Naples and we arrive in Rome. Somehow a room is rented in a pension, an attractive room, sunny, cheap and surrounded by green leaves and flowers. A cheerful, fat and friendly concierge keeps urging us to go somewhere important which we finally understand to be the Vatican.

It is Sunday, church bells are ringing, there are interesting ruins, sunshine and flowers everywhere. It is lovely but we cannot linger, we have to go quickly before we run out of money! Tutsica and I promise each other that someday we will return to lovely Italy.

Mama, with her eighth sense, a migratory instinct probably bestowed on her by Abraham, Isaac and Jacob—tribal ancestors she is always invoking—leads the way by train through the snow-covered rocks, called the Alps, which are very frightening, onward across exquisite, flower strewn plains, to Paris.

Ah, Paris! Tutsica and I know all about Paris. Not for nothing had we soaked up all those French tragedies and romances and we are well aware that a Rudolpho or a Mimi could be encountered on any one of these tree-lined boulevards any minute. All we have to do is to walk around long enough or sit down on a bench and wait.

The Wretched of the Earth—and Me

Paris c. 1919

The room we occupy in a cheap hotel, not far from the *Gare du Nord*, is large and airy. Most amazing of all is the miraculous indoor plumbing. Here is a box, containing a never-ending quantity of water, suspended above, and all you have to do is pull a chain to release a controlled river cleverly rushing where it is intended to go. I am convinced it is the most elegant, ingenious system devised by the human brain. If only they had those in Roumania!

But thinking of Roumania is no good, for we have other troubles. Our tourist class fare to Naples has been more than we could afford and after putting aside money for our *shiftscarten* (boat-fare) there is very little left over. We cannot afford meals in restaurants. In fact we only have a little left for emergencies. Our sausage has become rank in the soft sweet Italian air; our 'nothings' are reduced to crumbs.

"*Kinder*," says Mama, "It is more important to have a place where to lay your head. *Got vilt helfen*."

The next day, sure enough, God helps us. Tutsica and I find an *étalage de primeur* (first fruits stand) on the street and we are able to buy some really succulent, sweet turnips from the fruit peddler for just a few *sous*.

Got vilt helfen

These, peeled and well-chewed, served us as food for a couple of days. We had the imperishable green gage plums for dessert.

"It was just like manna," says Tutsica, well satisfied with herself. On the third day Mama thinks it urgent for us to make a short visit to the hotel dining room. Here, I justify Mama's confidence in my French. I say "Du pain, s'il vous plait" and I hear repeated through to the kitchen "Du pain, du pain, du pain," and I'm very proud.

In the meantime we are slated to be the principals in one of those dramas that happen only in French novels of an early period (and to emigrants on their way to *America*).

Our *shiftscarten*

Mama follows a mysterious time-table of her own, and the day finally arrives which she regards as auspicious for breaking the trail to the New World.

"Stay in the room, *Kinder*," she says to us one morning, "I'm going out to buy our *shiftscarten*." Why she had not bought the tickets before, she did not explain. She left and came back not with the tickets, but with a man, a man with a black moustache, a Roumanian, who was some sort of travel agent. He bows low, he kisses hands, even mine, and takes us into the dining room to buy us drinks. He buys a delicious frothy, pink one for me, and shows his teeth all the time in a sickly smile. With my innocent childish perspicacity I distrust him from the moment I see him. Not Mama! She gives him all our money to buy tickets and he makes off with our fate and our hopes in his pocket.

He is gone for a long time. The atmosphere becomes tense. We don't look at each other. Tutsica and I start hanging out of the windows in a vain attempt to conjure the figure of our 'travel agent' coming up the street.

We keep up our watch for what seems like hours. Eventually even Mama begins to worry. She looks dreadful, pacing the room with her arms hugging her chest. I'm afraid she is going to cry. I am angry to see her suffer and I mentally admonish her. "Didn't our cousins tell us to be careful? Don't you remember they told us not to trust strangers with our money, especially Roumanians?" Perhaps she had even been told that Roumanians had the reputation of being the world's greatest confidence artists, but—here he is, coming up the street, toiling up the stairs, shepherding us into the dining room for drinks and explaining how hard it is to get tickets.

"You are leaving in two days, Madame, on the *Leontine* from Le Havre to New York. That is the only route I could get." Then he departs, bowing, kissing hands and wishing us *"Bon Voyage."* We follow him to the door of the hotel, our eyes brimming over with relief and affection.

Our shiftscarten

"What a nice man," says Mama unashamedly wiping away tears of deliverance.

Le Havre is the end of the line for many emigrants, like ourselves. Money is really low now and during the night of our arrival in port, as we drag our belongings about in two cheap suitcases, we see many a family bedded down on the sidewalks. Some, snuggled into *perines* (down-filled comforters) ignoring social disapprobation, will be warm and cozy all night, while we, in what had been our elegant suits—now somewhat stained and travel creased—wander around looking for a bench. We don't find one and huddle on the ground on a bit of grass under a tree, leaning on each other, hungry and tired.

"Sit up, *Kinder*," says Mama. "Put your head on my shoulder, Malica, and sleep a little, but don't lie down. It isn't nice!"

The *Leontine* takes seven days to get to New York. Our accommodation is steerage—large areas all covered with some sort of beds or camp cots—and, on one side, long tables for eating. The meals are abominable, even to my usually good appetite, the meat being particularly vile. The air below seems thick with all sorts of evil smells and we escape to the crowded decks above as much as we can. The hellish spectacle of hundreds laying half undressed on their cots, for there was nowhere to sit, makes me very unhappy and I try to project myself into the future.

"What will we do in America?" I ask Tutsica. "I want to go to University!" I announce, skipping a few stages.

"Oh no, you won't be able to do that. There won't be any money. We'll just lead the lives of *bohêmes*."

(Poor Tutsica! She was prophetic, for only a few weeks later, arbitrarily renamed Annie by the sisters, she was a full member of the proletariat, punching a time card from 8 to 6 in a hat factory on Wellington Street, Toronto.)

When we finally arrive in New York, everyone is unloaded at Ellis Island, the small island in New York harbour used as an immigration centre. They call it the "Castle Garden" and I love it immediately. It is very spacious and has interminably long corridors along which we are propelled inexplicably from one official at a desk, to another similarly seated. "But that is as it should be," I say to myself. The long corridors, the very large sheds where we sit for hours waiting we know not what for, the official smell, (a mix of people, old luggage and antiseptic) is just right for a country that is rich, great and has the means to erect such buildings and staff them with important-looking officials.

The Wretched of the Earth—and Me

Ellis Isle c. 1919

And they supply us with all the food we need—for nothing.

Such food! Mountains of white bread (my favorite food), and very good *wurst*, the right kind of sausage smelling only of garlic! And those ridiculous breakfasts—cake-like confections called 'corn flakes.' A delicacy by itself, which the Americans, in their immense wealth, drown in milk and sugar. Plates, piled high with delicious eatables are ours at every meal. At the counter, where we pick up our food, there is a young man serving who is always cheerful and smiling. It bodes well for the future. I am quite happy at the "Castle Garden" and have the greatest confidence in the American way of doing things. Maybe I'll even get to go to University!

Then, one day, the greatest tragedy that could befall an immigrant family falls on our heads.

The Hebrew Immigrant Aid Society

A slight, little woman, apparently an American, addresses me in what I took to be half Yiddish and half English but which was actually Yiddish as spoken in America.

"Tell me," she inquires sweetly "Why do they want to send you back to Roumania?"

Waves of shock, of sorrow, of despair break over my head. I hadn't known anything and why does she ask me? I run to Mama. I run to Tutsica. They had known all about it and they have no comforting words to say. A blanket of sadness and gloom descends on our little group and we hang on to each other, a heap of sorrow.

Mama frightens me more by taking out her prayer book, reading for hours at a time, her lips forming the difficult Hebrew words silently.

"If she keeps reading her *Seder* it is like sitting *Shiva* for the dead. It is all over. We are going to be sent back. Where to?" I agonize to Tutsica. Mother moves around every day, absent-mindedly, silently, withdrawn, only her pale blue eyes fixed in a wide stare showing her anxiety. We walk around, a doomed trio, feeling as though misfortune has singled us out from the crowd, as for an execution.

"What did we do wrong, Mama?" I insist. "Why are they sending us back? What are they going to do to us? When is it going to happen?" In my agony, I want it to be over quickly.

Had I but known, salvation lay with the little American lady! She of the broken Yiddish, who was an angel in disguise, sent directly, no doubt, by my mother's interceding tribal ancestors, Abraham, Jacob and Isaac.

She was a social worker and a representative of the Hebrew Immigrant Aid Society, (H.I.A.S.)

We were not alone in our tragedy. For decades, thousands who had come to the United States and Canada, after agonizing journeys, having spent their last penny, their last ounce of strength getting there, were detained, then returned to the country from which they had come.

The Wretched of the Earth—and Me

Then in 1892, a small group of Jewish people in New York City, who originated from the same town or village in the 'old country,' organized an association for the purpose of providing burial for the Jews who died on Ellis Island. That is what they were—benevolent burial societies. When they looked around "Castle Garden," they decided to help the living and organized the H.I.A.S.

They interceded with the immigration authorities on behalf of thousands who were barred from entry, they had agents meet the immigrants and act as interpreters, guides and counsellors. They aided the despatch of newcomers and their baggage to their destinations and they issued a card with instructions in Yiddish and English to all new arrivals which read:

> BEWARE!
> DON'T GIVE ANY MONEY
> BE CAREFUL OF YOUR TICKETS!
> THE JEWISH IMMIGRANT AID SOCIETY WILL HELP
> YOU FREE OF CHARGE IN EVERYTHING YOU NEED!
> APPLY TO OUR MEN IN THE IMMIGRATION BUILDINGS.

Joseph Kage "With Faith and Thanksgiving"

The Society even helped non-Jewish immigrants.

What did *we* do wrong?

There were many reasons why immigrants were detained and deported: non-continuous journey; insufficient funds; improper passports; medical reasons, etc. Ours was sin number one, 'non-continuous journey.' We should have gone directly to Quebec City or St. John's. Therefore the immigration authorities are going to send us back in order for us to start all over again and come to the right port. It is a paper game for them. It is life and death for us! We were rejected.

In those days the heartbreak of the rejected immigrants cried out, even in the newspapers:

> Brothers, it is a question of life and death....If we are sent back, we have nothing left to do but to throw ourselves into the ocean......We beg of you

The Hebrew Immigrant Aid School

mercy....We request you to help us secure here a place of rest where we can settle down to earn our bread... and to become honest and useful citizens and not to be deported.

Jewish Daily Eagle, Montreal 1921

The H.I.A.S. obtained lists of detained immigrants; these, and the reasons for detention, were forwarded to the head office. Contact was made with relatives and telegrams were sent.

Such a telegram is despatched to my sisters in Toronto and in a few days my brother-in-law, Willy, appears; tall, slim he is declared very handsome by Mama.

Together, Willy and the angel from the H.I.A.S. cause the gates of "Castle Garden" to swing open. We are released to the outside world.

Willy's first act is to buy us ice-cream sodas and chewing gum, thus transforming us instantly into native Americans.

We arrive in Toronto a few days later to find everything is wonderful.

Toronto c. 1919

The Wretched of the Earth—and Me

My married sisters are truly beautiful, Rosie's modest flat at 137 Major Street is palatial. Toronto, in June, 1919, is paradise itself.

Everyone was so happy to see us and so full of praise for Mama's bravery. But not a word was said of the missing one, she who had blazed the way earlier, my sister Dora.

It was Dora who pioneered the road from Rasca to Toronto. Dora, who because of a mysterious indiscretion committed at age 15, had been sent off to a far-away relative in Toronto, in 1910.

Dora and Giorgiu

Dora kept on appearing and disappearing in my childhood, leaving incomplete images. It was very difficult for me to piece together the events which led to her being sent off across the seas, and of her return just a few years after leaving Roumania. Why had my father and mother been so angry with her?

When I was very young I once ventured on these obscure and perplexing grounds.

"What did sister Dora do, Mama?"

Mama grew very angry and her usual affectionate manner towards her *mezinke* (youngest one) turned to irritation.

"Never let me hear you talk about that. It isn't for you. Go and play!"

I soon learned that any mention of "Her in America" brought deep sighs from Mama—from the past a hint of *scandale*. *Scandale* was a word very much in vogue in those days. It meant not so much financial or political scandal, as personal misbehaviour. The nature of Dora's misbehaviour, of the "scandale" she created, changed in my mind as the years passed and was only solved with time and adulthood.

* * * * * * *

Dora, the eldest, was a petite, extremely pretty, doll-like creature. She had eyes the color of forget-me-nots, a white skin kept free of freckles by a religious avoidance of the sun, and delicate, regular features framed by curly light brown hair shading into blond.

My mother and father, however, could take little joy in their lovely daughter. Beautiful as she might have been, she was equally saucy, immodest, flirtatious and disobedient at a time and place when children and adolescents obeyed their parents instantly.

"Keep out of here!" my father yells at here! "Keep out of the *kretchme* (the pub). This is no place for you."

The Wretched of the Earth—and Me

Dora c. 1919

Dora and Giorgia

Only men frequented the tavern. Women, presumably didn't drink, not in public anyway. Dora, however, had access to the area at the back of the counter and from that vantage point could watch the activities in the tavern.

Her main interest was men. It didn't matter whether they were old or young, handsome or ugly. She was as interested in the skilled workers from the local saw mill as she was in the few clerks who came in for a beer or the local schoolteacher.

As soon as there was an interesting man around her eyes would light up and in minutes she had lured him to the counter, engaged him in conversation and made him laugh. Her manner was flirtatious and teasing; her appraising glance gliding over the crowd while she speculated and fantasized. She paid no attention to strictures about not being allowed behind the counter nor in the private room kept for those who did not wish to mix in the common area with the locals.

What was she searching for?

Could she find it in this little hamlet?

Situated in the heavily-forested area of Roumania's northern province of Moldavia, Rasca owed its existence to a large saw mill, which cut the trees into marketable-sized lumber. It employed about 150 men who combined work in the mill with tilling a small plot of land. The settlement was arranged horse-shoe fashion around the mill and my parents ran the only tavern in the village. We lived on the premises. In front of the building a large, tramped down area was used on Sundays for the dancing of the *hora*. A ferris wheel, operated on that day only added to the excitement.

Four or five *klezmer* (musicians) were hired from the neighborhood, usually gypsies, who were the best interpreters of the type of music required for the *hora*. Mostly violins were played but frequently the music was augumented by shepherd's pipes, or the *kosba*, an instrument for accompaniment consisting of 8 to 12 pair of strings affixed to nails. The sounds are produced by plucking the strings with goose quills.

The music was fast, lively and merry, interspersed by calling out and *doinas*, those long and sad songs in which the singer describes his troubles to be shared by the dancers and the musicians whose mood changes accordingly to the melancholy and tearful.

Everyone came in their beautiful, treasured holiday wear, the men wearing tight unbleached cotton trousers and an embroidered linen shirt worn outside the pants, gathered at the waist by a long, wide brightly

The Wretched of the Earth—and Me

Dancing the Hora

cross-stitched sash and on their feet, *opinchi*, (home-made leather footwear, more or less like a short laced-up slipper). The women were even more magnificently attired in skirts of hand-loomed multi-colored threads, the wide sleeves of their linen blouses fairly doubled in thickness by the weight of brilliant embroidery, frequently accented with beads and sequins. A wide band, hand-woven in many colors encircled the waist and around the neck the girls wore thick ropes of beads.

How I envied the peasant girls their beads! They came in all shapes and colors, droplets and rivulets of magic tints. Most of all I loved the small seeds in strings of blue like the sky itself, or the shiny ropes of red like the poppies in the fields, or colored tender green like the grass in the meadows; or the sweet milky white ones and above all, the dainty pink, the pink of bleeding hearts in full bloom in the springtime. To top the fantasy they heaped on strings of *hormuz*, gold colored globules reflecting the movement of the dance and so light that singly they floated in the air with the wind.

We children were not allowed in the front during these goings on, officially that is. Unofficially, there was a great deal of peeping, of

Dora and Giorgia

borrowing of needle and thread or of tiny bits of mirror. There was tension on Sundays as well because of the noise and drinking.

Not everyone spent their time drinking.

I watched with worry and fear one Sunday as my father stonily eyed a local peasant from behind the wooden grill that protected the whole length of the bar. The peasant had drunk away all his money and was looking for a fight.

"*Jidan!*" he murmured in a drunken monotone,"*Jidan, Jidan!*" (Dirty Jew). Father stood still, glaring with murder in his eyes but there was nothing he could do. We were glad when the women took their shoes off towards the end of the day, slung them over their shoulders to save the leather and led the long way home.

The rest of the week was quiet and we could enjoy our peaceful life again.

For Dora, however there was only boredom and frustration. Her daily routine revolved around her household chores, reading when a book was available, and some interest with growing flowers provided it was done out of the sun. She embroidered a sampler in red cross stitching showing a young woman with a cap and a long dress carrying a tray loaded with presumably highly-breakable breakfast dishes. It read: *"Ube forzicht elle nicht das geshire vert licht zubricht."* (Take care, these dishes are easily broken). There was also German influence in the country, mainly in things technological; the maintenance engineers at the saw mill were German; father imported beer from Germany for them; and the best crafted items were those which bore the stamp "Made in Germany." We still have a pair of scissors in the family over a hundred years old marked "J.A.Henckels."

There was not much else for Dora, no music except for the Sunday gathering, no art and no social life. She could only wait for marriage.

She refused to wait. She refused to be squeezed into the mould of a marriageable daughter in a small town. She knew what to expect for she had seen it around her. Mama and Papa would have to employ the local part-time *shotchen*, the marriage broker. This character would finally come up with an unsuitable prospective husband, a widower likely, short, elderly and with a squint. Such a one was chosen for father's younger sister and didn't she die in childbirth only one year after the wedding and all his awful impoverished relatives turned up swarming all over and claiming each of the deceased's household items?

The Wretched of the Earth—and Me

Dora had gathered all this from parental conversations and she knew, moreover, that a dowry would be asked for, as well, by that awful man and there would be humiliating bickerings. You simply could not trust parents to find a handsome, exciting young man for a husband in Rasca. True there were very few exciting young men to choose from but there were very handsome young gypsy lads to pass the time with, if one was not too frightened or shy. Dora was not shy nor did she lack courage. She was fifteen when she created the *scandale* that shook Rasca.

The news of the disaster broke early on a Monday morning.

Little girl voices shrilled the news.

"Mama, Dora isn't in her bed. She didn't sleep here last night. Mama, Dora has run away."

Tutsica and I knew Dora had been seen. Dora had been observed. In a few hours, the whole horror of her action unravelled itself before the stunned family. Dora had run away with the most attractive of the gypsy lads, Georgiu, he of the curly hair, flashing black eyes and very bold manner. He played the fiddle every Sunday for the *Hora*.

Papa was bitter; devastated.

"We'll leave her where she is. She is no longer our daughter. She'll get what she deserves."

Between sobs, Mama pleaded: "Hershel, don't. She's our little girl. He will beat her. Go bring her back."

After three days Papa brought the unrepentant Dora home.

Thus, sorrow, misfortune and gloom descended and settled on our house. Dora was shut in a room by herself. Mama wept continuously, and urchins from undisciplined families peeked into our windows and waited outside for the woman of easy virtue to make an appearance.

We were disgraced!

Father, bowed down under the terrible weight of what he proclaimed to be God's punishment, prayed for days on end, then announced we must sit *shiva* for Dora.

Tutsica filled me in with details.

When someone dies, we sit *shiva* as a sign of mourning for a dear relative. The bereaved darken a room, cover the mirrors, take off their shoes and sit on the floor giving full reign to their grief for the period of one week. During that time, conversation takes places in whispers only, some meager nourishment is taken, no business or household duties are attended to and one may read only prayer books.

Dora and Giorgia

Daily, if possible at sunset, a *minyan*, a basic congregation of 10 is convened to say the twilight prayers in the *shiva* room. One sits *shiva* for living people as well. When a son or daughter transgresses the basic rules of the Jewish community, usually by marrying a non-Jew, the family sits *shiva* and the son or daughter is henceforth regarded as dead.

However, it was difficult to sit *shiva* for Dora and pronounce her dead when she was in the next room.

Better to send her to *America*. A distant relative was discovered in Toronto, Canada and, with few tears of regret, she was packed off.

For those of us left behind, life continued to be sad. Our home remained veiled in grief and disgrace but the little village was ecstatic. Such excitement! So many things to talk about, whisper about, dig into and chew over. Such good yarns for the gossip looms. It could last for years.

Mama and Papa retreated into themselves, did not appear outside much, were covered with shame. The situation was particularly hard on the next two girls, my sisters Mali and Rosie. (There was some confusion about names in the family. Next to Dora the eldest, there was Mali and Rosie. Being only 6 years old when they left, I really did not know them well until I arrived in Canada in 1919. The next twosome was Tutsica and myself—originally named Amelia but called Malica for short. Thus there were two Mali's in the family, which was resolved when I arrived in Canada by my being renamed Minnie.)

Mali and Rosie, in no time at all would reach a critical marriageable age; these, too, the village gossip painted with the colors of their sister's adventurism. Two years later, off they went as well, following Dora to Toronto, Canada.

It was at this time that Mama suggested: "Do you know what, Hershel? Let us go too, I mean to *America*." But the *scandale* about Dora was fading somewhat and life was too good for the family to pull up roots and leave.

We remained.

I was getting older, around six years of age, attending school and enjoying myself. There was a grocery store next door. Clarissa Michelson, the grocer's daughter was my friend and we played together. Mother baked on Fridays and lovely smells filled the house. There was no butcher shop but I would be sent to the *shoichet* (the man who did the ritual killing) with a chicken for the Sabbath and from time to time beef

The Wretched of the Earth—and Me

or lamb appeared on the table, killed locally and divided among the Jewish inhabitants. As we had no ice, everything had to be eaten fresh—no hardship!

In the spring we had green onions, cucumbers, radishes and new garlic out of our garden. These would be chopped into a bowl and eaten with cottage cheese and thick, sour cream. In the summer there were wild strawberries and lots of raspberries for the table and for jam. Every now and then men came from the mountain areas bringing brook trout in beds of woven pine and in the fall there would be goose which my father smoked by simply climbing up to the roof and hanging it down the chimney flue.

In the autumn we sometimes made a simple supper of walnuts (which were so new and fresh we children would peel the skin off the meat), accompanied by apples, pears and Mama's bread. There were marvellous cheeses and *mamaliga*, (corn meal mush) although widely regarded as peasant food, was popular in our family. It was eaten with sweet, drawn butter, *branza* (goat cheese) and *urda* (made from ewe's milk).

We put down many sorts of jam in the fall but the favorite was *povidla*, a sort of prune butter. This was cooked down, in a large cauldron, not in the kitchen but outside and was stored away for the winter in every receptacle imaginable including enamel ware. Apples, stored in barrels, and root vegetables, were kept fresh in our own huge wine cellars.

Rasca had its own traditions for home-made remedies. A 'freckle cream' was produced locally, while baths in walnut leaves were good for rheumatism. Tutsica and I were sent off to a farmer's cottage twice a week for this cure. We waited while walnut leaves were gathered, placed in a wooden tub and hot water poured over them. We then soaked ourselves in this aromatic concoction, and then traipsed home, if not healthier, at least scented and clean.

It was also in Rasca that Mama found enough cabbage roses to make jam out of the petals. This came out thick, creamy and, when opened during the winter, brought back the scent of a rose garden in June.

There was many a bonus for living near the saw-mill.

"Come, *Kinderlich*, (children) we are going to the baths!" Mama would say on a Friday afternoon, after the *Shabbat* cooking was done and the whole house was tidy and clean.

We then walked over to the saw mill and mother made her way amidst noise and confusion to a room where there were two, huge—to me—porcelain tubs and plenty of hot water for us to splash in.

Dora and Giorgia

To top it all, emanating from the saw-mill generator, electric light (a miracle in that age and area), spread its blessing, lighting up the house and the village.

It was this quiet life that Dora shattered once more by her letter announcing that she is returning for a visit, scarcely four years after leaving Roumania forever.

Dora's Toronto

At 6.30 in the morning of a Monday in October in the good year 1910, it is both cold and dark as Dora trudges to work. The immigrant Jewish population in Toronto clusters close to the factory district of Spadina-Adelaide-King Streets. They live on Augusta Avenue, Dundas Street (called Agnes), and even on Center Avenue and Simcoe Street. With the shops so near to the residential areas, it is not too difficult to walk to work and save carfare. Although the day is just beginning, Dora is tired and her heart is crying out against her lot. Yesterday she wept as she wrote home to her parents in Roumania:

My dear mother and father, my dear sisters:

I have to write to say that I am very lonely for you all and life is very hard here in Canada. I am living by myself now in a small room on Agnes Street for which I pay $2.00 a week. I only have a bed, a chair and a wash stand and the wallpaper is yellow and cracked. In the wintertime it is very cold and sometimes I go to bed with most of my clothes on. The heat comes from a "self heater" which is a round stove kept in the hall downstairs and pipes are supposed to bring heat from it to my room but the landlady is very stingy and puts very little coal in the stove so that it doesn't give much heat. Now that the weather is warm it really

Dora's Toronto

doesn't matter so much but I'm scared for next winter. My balabusta (landlady) lets me cook some soup with meat on her stove downstairs sometimes, but very often I eat in my room. I keep a loaf of bread and I buy maslines (black olives) and wurst (sausage).

Dear Mama, I have trouble washing my clothes. Now that the weather is fine I wash them in a small basin in the yard. I have to carry water from the kitchen and my landlady gets cranky. I have no iron but I borrow one from a girl in the next room. I get $6.00 a week and after I pay for the room and buy some food I don't have much left. During the winter time I went to night school to learn to speak English. It is very hard as nobody at work speaks English, only Yiddish and when I asked if there is anybody who speaks French in the shop they made fun of me. The girls and men at work don't like me. They think I give myself airs. I don't like them either and I don't care what they think of me. They have no education and not one of them has heard of Emile Zola. There is nothing about which I want to talk to them. Some of them are dirty and they have no manners.

Now that summer is here, there are many places to go to like Hanlan's Point. It is an island. It is very pretty there with green trees, grass, and funny

The Wretched of the Earth—and Me

Hanlan's Point, Toronto, c. 1910

rides, something like our ferris wheel only many more and of different sorts. You have to pay to go on them. I like better a place called High Park and

High Park, Toronto, c. 1910

Dora's Toronto

The Canadian National Exhibition, c. 1910

The Comique Theatre, Toronto, c. 1910

people take food with them and sun themselves and eat. But I have very little money to go to these places and really no friends. There are fine stores called Simpsons and Eatons where, on Saturdays, you can walk around and look at all the lovely things. Some of the girls steal. They think nobody is looking but there are jandarmes in plain clothes watching. A girl from our shop was caught once and the police took her away. When she had a trial, she came before a lady judge. Any women who get into trouble come before this lady judge. The judge let the girl go free but she had to promise never to go into this store again.

I work in a millinery shop making hats. Everyone wears hats, one for the summer and one for the winter. They are not made by hand, like at home Mama, but on machines and we have to work very fast and make many hats a day. We work on piece-work, everyone does a different part of the hat, but we don't get paid by the piece, but by the week. Some workers say we should get paid by the piece; we would make more money that way. I am sad most of the time and miss you all so much. I dream about you all and of being back in Roumania.

I close this letter with love and longing.

Your loving daughter and sister,

Dora

Dora's Toronto

A great many immigrants arrived in Toronto in 1910 and there is much demand for housing and clothing and light industry, particularly the needle trades, is very busy. For the rich and even for some native Canadians of the working class, life is fine. One can take an excursion from Toronto to Port Dalhousie in the summer time, the *Trillium* runs to the islands:

CENTER, WARDS
AND
HANLAN'S POINT

where well-to-do Canadians maintain lovely summer homes. A sightseeing motor coach tours the city, making a ten-mile round trip for $1.00.

Scarborough Beach provides amusements, sunning and swimming and one dresses up in one's best Sunday clothes to throng the wooden sidewalks and the amusement places. The Royal Canadian Yacht Club has been in existence since 1854, curling is engaged in by the Scottish-born settlers, and there is a bicycle club called the Toronto Wanderers. During the years 1910 to 1914 Sir Henry Pellat built his castle, Casa Loma on the Davenport hill and when it was finished it had its own telephone system, a marble swimming pool and gold fawcets in the bathrooms. French perfume sprinkled from Lady Pellat's shower. The castle can be viewed from outside, and going up Spadina Avenue to the hill provides a Sunday outing for the poor people.

Woodbine track is available for the rich to indulge in the sometimes newly-acquired passion for horse racing and the meat packers, the contractors and the share owners of railway stock are doing a good business. In 1910 there are beautiful homes on Wellington Street and Government House stands majestically on the corner of King and Simcoe Street.

Little boys go swimming in the Don River.

Dora knows very little about all this, for life can be dull and cruel for a 'greenie' compelled to make a living in a sweat shop. She is only 17 years old but she feels aged and tired before the day has even begun and she is permeated with hatred for her life. She hates getting out of bed on a cold and wet morning. She hates her mean room. She hates it when she gets home at night because she is too tired to do anything but eat and go to bed. She even hates Sundays because the next day is Monday and the beginning of a new week of slavery.

The Wretched of the Earth—and Me

Above all she hates her jeering and taunting work mates, particularly Mendl. She certainly made a mistake when she turned Mendl down, that time he asked her to go walking in Queen's Park.

"Oh God, how I hate America," she sighs to herself throwing all of North America in one pot of iniquity. "But I should hurry a bit or I'll be late to punch the time-clock and get 'docked' (have money deducted from wages) for it. When she arrives she is greeted with the usual chorus.

"Nu, Pritze, (Aristocratic Lady!) what exciting things did you do yesterday?" Ida, the girl sitting next to Dora and who is said to be making eyes at Mendl, is always teasing and accusing her of being a snob.

"Tell me, Mendl," says Ida" who is more stuck up, Dvorah, the *Pritze*, or Henry, the bookkeeper?"

"Oh him! Friday when I said 'Good morning' to him he didn't even answer. He talks only to the floor."

"And she talks only to the sky."

Mendle claims,"They are so stuck up, that even if they got together they wouldn't have anything to do with each other because they're too used to turning up their noses at everybody. Henry's too stuck up to talk to Dvorah and Dvorah is too stuck up to talk to a man who isn't a *graf* (a nobleman) and there are no *grafs* in the shop."

At noon, Ida calls softly into the office and gets Henry out. Then she pushes him roughly towards Dora."Here she is, talk to her, say 'Hello.'"

Henry flees, but not before he has had a good look at the pretty petite girl (now) with freckles and the blue eyes. He waits for her after work, does not talk to her but watches her. The truth is that Henry is not a snob but merely shy. However, on the third day of watching her leave the shop, he approaches her—she was well aware of what was going on—and walks her home. They go steady.

Henry Shilling, British born, a book-keeper, though still of the working class, is an improvement on the uneducated, crude and largely unattractive lot of young men she sees around.

"If he asks you to marry him, you will say yes," she advises herself.

Mrs. Henry Shilling

And so Dora marries Henry Shilling. The situation improves. She can stay home from work. Instead of a single room, there is a flat on Augusta Avenue and her landlady, Mrs. Bregman, takes a motherly interest in the 'upstairs couple.'

Dora goes shopping frequently, dresses with more elegance, learns to cook Canadian dishes. However, she finds the environment still drab, there is no social life, no sophistication, no culture.

One year later, a little girl is born and Dora feels the never-ending household chores like ropes around her body. She feels restless again as though she has been miscast in a role she has not chosen for herself nor desired. Definitely, she feels out of time and place.

"The baby," she complains to Mrs.Bregman, "wants only her bottle and her father wants only his paper and slippers at the end of the day." She has no patience with either.

Henry is kind, or perhaps gullible. He is also a good saver. A year after the little girl is born, succumbing to a great campaign lasting weeks, of begging and prodding, he gives Dora enough money for a one-way ticket for herself and the child to visit her parents in Roumania.

To my mother and father her return to Rasca is a disastrous storm sweeping into their lives, not wholly unexpected but dreaded nonetheless.

To Tutsica and me, however, her arrival is like that of a fairy godmother. Her gifts were white dresses of *broderie anglaise* deeply scalloped, accompanied by white underslips, garments new in our lives and 'gold' extension bracelets. Dora dresses my blond hair up in 'Mary Pickford' curls and Mama's larder now includes a heavenly food called shredded coconut. Some bananas, brought green, were retained by curious custom officers 'for examination.'

Life became very exciting for us once more and difficult.

Dora organized a literary circle and a few young girls join in the hope of meeting young men. Then two married men join up and the girls drop out. Finally Dora is left with a circle of men only, all claiming to be ardent students of literature, until my father becomes worried.

"Stop it," he insists. "What kind of books are you reading there? The government will become interested. It isn't good for me."

Father had a license to sell tobacco which was most difficult to obtain and it was not advisable to get the government interested in our tavern.

Mother was worried for other reasons. She had tried to keep Dora down to the level of behaviour prevalent in Rasca but it was very difficult for Dora was very resourceful, as on the day when Mama suggested I accompany her for a walk by the river. Dora, who was not alone, allowed me to tag along, but not for long. Soon, I was back home.

"What are you doing here?" snapped Mama.

"Dora sent me to bring her a glass of water, I have to bring it to her."

My main worry was how I was going to carry the water so that it would not spill while getting back to the woods, where Dora was strolling with a gentleman.

Finding Dora's behaviour as hard to control as the waters of the little brook at the back of our property, and business being slow, my father carried through a long-planned change, bought another tavern and moved his family and possessions to the nearby town of Falticeni.

For a while, the storm abated. I was able to go to school, there was a girl to help with the work, Dora was busy investigating her environment and the pub was making money.

But the time unhappily was August 1914.

A lone soldier, sounding a call to arms on a trumpet in the middle of the night—why in the middle of the night? Roumanian sense of urgency? It shattered our quiet world, ushering in World War I and mobilization in Falticeni.

There being few newspapers and only the most rudimentary means of communication, it was essential that the the trumpeter's call be heard by all concerned. It was heard by our family and brought immediate dread and great anxiety—for Dora, fear that her lines of communication to Canada were cut for good—for father trembling for his business and expecting all sorts of "government foolishness."

We did not have long to wait. Simultaneously with the declaration of war, prohibition was declared and a few short days after, government officials descended on our now closed tavern. Showing a piece of paper as authority, they proceeded to spill wine, *tsuica* (Roumanian brandy), beer, and even precious imported liquors into the gutter. Staves were broken in on wine casks, the necks of tall, important-looking bottles knocked off on the sidewalk and, with gusto, everything was emptied on the side of the road. As the gutters soon ran red and gold with the precious fluids, the gathering crowd of spectators rushed for cups and vessels. My father looked on, dazed and stupified as though it was his life's blood that was streaming down the gutter. Not quite comprehending the madness surrounding him, attempting in vain to stop them, he refused indignantly the offer of a piece of paper, a receipt.

"The government will pay," they said and such is the faith of the bureaucracy in its own edicts, no matter how nonsensical, that they were indignant at my father's lack of trust.

"But you have a receipt," they insisted, not understanding this very ungrateful man who was staring in bewilderment from the piece of paper tendered him to the wine rushing down the gutter.

It seems that father was right.

Nothing was ever heard of reimbursement. The piece of paper, representing the hard work of a lifetime, was worthless. Two years later, impoverished, prematurely aged and heartbroken, my father died.

As the war progressed the Roumanian government favored us again with their attention and we were sent an army colonel to be quartered in the only spare room we had.

He dwelt there—attended by a batman—long enough for Dora to get well acquainted with him and his romantic sky-blue cape that all army officers dashed around in. When he departed, she went along, leaving her little girl, now four years old, with us.

The time was now 1917 and world-shaking events were being played out, reaching even Falticeni

When the Roumanian colonel left with his regiment he was replaced by our brave allies, the Czar's army. Suddenly the town was full of Russian soldiers and an air-force unit found itself a field just outside Falticeni. We never saw any planes actually flying but some were seen on the ground, idle tongues claiming that they were being towed around for lack of fuel. At any rate we now had Russian air-force personnel quartered in our large former barroom.

The population happily took the Russians to their hearts and had no trouble profiting from their presence. Women began wearing tall fur hats, cossack style, filched from off the heads of lovers, it was said. Several

The Wretched of the Earth—and Me

demi-mondaines were riding around the town in handsome carriages, accompanied by members of the higher echelons of the Russian army.

Those who were not young or beautiful set up tables on the sidewalks selling pathetic decks of playing cards and sunfloweer seeds by the glass.

Sister Dora returned resplendent in a nurse's uniform, having just joined the Roumanian Red Cross and was followed around town by a retinue of admiring Russian officers.

The Russians quartered with us were quiet and courteous and always seemed to be wanting our approval, worried lest they do something considered as *ni culturni* (gross). They were not to be regarded as soldiers, they insisted and wanted to be known by their first names.

"Call me Boris" one pleaded.

"Call me uncle Vasili" said another, and they brought out yellowing photographs of young children. "A little girl like yourself," to show us.

Frequently and shyly they produced loaves of fine white bread, for the air force had white flour and quantities of tea, "*Pentru* Madame," a much appreciated addition to our frequently bare cupboard, for food was scarce and bread and meat rationed. They seemed so happy to be near a real family. Were they reassessing themselves in the light of the revolution which even then was shaking their mother country?

But the Roumanian-Russian alliance was breaking apart. The Russians wanted out of the war to pursue their own struggles against the autocracy of Tzarism.

The air-force, encamped around Falticeni, carried through its own little revolt; a colonel was shot to death and a Soviet of the revolutionary air-force was set up, the meeting taking place in our former barroom.

After the meeting, I was sent out to buy huge quantities of red ribbon, all that I could find in the little dry goods store across the street, Dora and I did our revolutionary duty and made red ribbon bows for the whole committee.

In the evening there was a celebration marked by much playing of *balalaikas* and two men, fierce Cossacks, danced with knives in their teeth.

Very shortly after that, "Our brave allies," now the Red Army and their non-functioning planes, took off to attend to more important business on the home front.

The air-force had some vehicles, but the army which followed them two days later, seemed to have none.

Mrs. Henry Shilling

The Red Army, c. 1917

Early in the morning, a rumour swept the streets:
"The Russian Army is Marching Home."
Everyone took up positions of vantage to watch the army file by.
"Will there be music? Will they carry their swords?"
I was familiar with the uniforms of the Roumanian lieutenants, who carried clanging swords and looked very dashing in their lovely light blue tunics with matching capes worn jauntily over one shoulder.
"Will the officers ride at the head on white horses?" I asked.
Finally the Russian Army oozed in, an unorganized mass filling the street and spiling over unto the sidewalk. There was no marching, no formation, no timing and no music. They walked wearily, just dragging themselves onward, limping, some carrying stout branches to help them put one foot in front of the other.
"Is this an army Mama? Are these soldiers?
" Soldiers, are just men my child."
They limped on, dressed in a ragged array of odds and ends, bits of uniform, black, baggy 'Turkish' trousers available in towns, long white cotton pants of the Roumanian peasantry, unbelievably dirty and ragged.

The Wretched of the Earth—and Me

For shoes, half rubbers tied on with rope, torn *opinchi* from the countryside, and old leggings wound around the feet and secured with lengths of cloth or rope which floped around a great deal and which the men stopped to tie or replace.

For the first time I saw Orientals "from Turkestan," the same person said. "they're marvellous horsemen." They wore flat, fur-type hats, baggy trousers, were very short in stature and seemed even worse off than the others. They walked painfully, sort of rolling from side to side.

Where were the army boots, the uniforms, the rifles, the trucks, the horses for the men from Turkestan? Where were the officers?

This army exuded tragedy, hunger and sickness. I shivered in fright.

"Where did they come from, Mama? Why are they like that? Are they tired, Mama?"

"Yes, they are very tired, my child and hungry. They should stop and rest."

They didn't stop.They dragged along, ragged, weary, hungry and the population watching, weeping inwardly in their pity and sympathy.

In time I learned that what I was witnessing, was part of the huge, mostly peasant army, starving, ill-equipped, heeding Lenin's call of "Peace, bread and freedom" and "voting with their feet" to end the war.

The war ended for Roumania as well.

Dora took her little girl and went off to Bucharest, to new adventures, new horizons.

It was months, however, after my father's death, before Mama recovered somewhat from the blows visited on her by the Roumanian government, fate, and Dora.

"*Kinder*," she announced to us one day, "We are leaving. We'll go to *America*."

My Toronto

Nineteen-nineteen, it was a warm June day, the June of our arrival in Toronto. In the garden of my sister Rosie's home on Major Street I was examining the growing things, searching for the same plants that grew in Roumania. There was a small lilac bush in the 'yard' next door (why do they call a garden a 'yard' here?) and the dandelions looked the same as at home but there were no pansies and no bleeding hearts, my favorites.

"People don't seem to have much time for flowers here," I say to myself. I am paraphrasing Mama, who is already talking of "Here in Canada" (although she always calls it *America*) and "At home in Roumania." So far she finds things better in Roumania which leads to many arguments. But the morning is perfect. I am happy in the sunshine amidst the greenery and the soft air.

I loved my sister's house on Major Street. Across the road there was a four-story apartment building, "Where rich people live, even a clothing manufacturer," my brother-in-law Willy explained with proper awe.

The street was quiet and tall chestnut trees in bloom spread their greenery along the whole avenue all the way to the corner of College Street where Mr. M. Koffler, a distant cousin mother claimed, owned the drug store which dispensed strawberry ice cream cones for 5 cents each. This drug store, one or two generations later, was to become Shoppers Drug Mart.

At the moment I was the only one still living at 137 Major Street. Some modifications to our little family had been made. Only weeks after our arrival Tutsica-Anne came home from work one day, to find me sad and bewildered. Rosie wouldn't explain.

"C'est la mère..." I began.

"Mais ou est notre mère?" Anne demanded.

"Elle s'en va avec un homme des lunettes et moustachu," I replied in my rapidly-rusting French.

It was true. A marriage of convenience was being arranged for Mama and in a week's time she had moved to Palmerston Avenue and Anne was to go with her within a few days.

The Wretched of the Earth—and Me

At this moment, however the arrival of my sister Molly made me very happy. Molly was very beautiful and I adored her. She had perfect features, green eyes, a delicate narrow straight nose, high cheek bones and small, even teeth framed by perfect lips which were often curled up in a smile.

She always had a friend, a young man or even an older one, who wanted to tag along and occasionally a little boy or girl who were supposed to be 'on a message' came as well. She was married and lived in an apartment, which was, socially, a level or two above a 'flat,' proving that her husband was a good earner. Also she didn't have to go to work. I loved being with her and here she was calling for me, alone this time. I was flattered at the attention.

"Come, Minnie," she said. "We will go find you a job."

I was 'Minnie' now, the Roumanian Malica being unsuitably close to her own name. Tutsica too had been renamed, an unexplainable 'Anne.'

"The papers come out at noon" she continued "and we'll be the first ones there."

'There' turned out to be a large paper-box manufacturing and printing plant on King Street, west of Spadina. Government regulations at that time forbade factory owners from hiring children under 16. From 14 to 16 years, however, one could work on a 'permit' based on the need of supporting oneself. I didn't have a permit and I was only 12. It now seemed that hiring a child who was under age, was really up to the foreman. This foreman took one look at sister Molly and hired me immediately. Nor did he inquire as to my age or ask for a permit.

"Are you sure you don't want a job?" he asked Molly. "My name is Scone. Now anytime you think you'd like some work...Drop in some time."

"No thank you. I'm married."

Molly moved off quickly and left me for I was to start work right away. The foreman crossed the office, motioned me to follow him and we entered the factory. I had never been in a factory before. I had never seen an electrically-driven machine before, not even in the saw mill in Rasca and I didn't know what to expect when he directed me into what was the print shop.

It was like descent into hell.

The entire floor space was occupied by various machines, crowded close to one another. Each one of them was different, and each more

My Toronto

King St., Toronto, factory, c. 1919

horrible than the next. Huge wheels turned small wheels. Square steel jaws opened and closed. Large round disks banged on each other, like cymbals. (They were actually printing presses of various sorts). One monster was so big, it would have taken a whole room to house it. It was grinding and whistling shrilly and throwing its thin steel arms up and down in a fearful way. Every one of these machines had its own dreadful noise and every one had its own timing for its noise. Through it all, tremenduously powerful leather belts whirled from floor to ceiling, more like arms, ready to grab and strike.

As if this wasn't enough, workers were actually putting their hands and arms into the gaping machines and withdrawing them just as they were about to be swallowed or crushed. They were 'feeding' the machines.

I was terrified.

The noise shook me to my toes. There was an evil smell as well, which, I learned afterwards, was a combination of printer's ink, machine oil, dust and hot air. A blue smoke visible through the weak light of naked bulbs, hung thick, right up to the far-off ceiling.

It was hell, without a doubt.

The Wretched of the Earth—and Me

The foreman, wearing a black leather apron, was leading me on. Making my way carefully, trying desperately not to get too near to any of the machines, I followed him. He brought me right to the room-sized monster and indicated that I was to climb high up to a seat in the middle of the machine itself, a long press.

"Go sit beside Frank" the foreman said. We were to regulate the fall of the printed matter, the young man, who was about 14 years old, on one side and I on the other.

I refused. I refused to sit there beside a 'man' I didn't know and I did not want to become part of this machine and I was fearful that it would grab me or that I would fall into its innards.

When the foreman left, I carefully climbed down and hung about the place, not knowing what to do next or how to find my way out.

"You'll get fired," yelled Frank after me. The man at the next machine also stopped me. "Watch out! He'll fire you."

"You're going to get fired! You'll be fired! Fired!"

The unfortunate expression threatened me from all sides. I did know the word 'fire.' It had to do with heat and flames. What can they mean? I glanced around fearfully for the fire and brimstone area. I was expecting Mr. Scone, with the leather apron, to come around and lead me there. Nothing would have surprised me in a place like this.

Mr. Scone, however, was very patient. He issued forth from one of those dark, noisy corners where a machine was groaning, moaning and gnashing. He nudged me, none too gently, back towards the press, saying "None of that now, back you go!" or words to that effect—I obeyed. Relieved that I wasn't going to be punished, I sat down as far away from Frank as possible, did my work as instructed but only until 5 o'clock. I had been informed that the hours were 8 to 5.

At 5 o'clock I climbed down and made my way to what was called the 'cloak room.' Mr. Scone caught me once more, and yelled something loudly, the tone of which meant more than displeasure. I quickly climbed back into my seat, attended to my work and watched impatiently for the power of the machine to be turned off. At 5.12 a loud bell rang, the power was turned off and everyone left their job.

Someone explained, later, that the working day was 8 to 5 but, to make sure that the workers didn't leave their machines before 5 to wash or change, 12 minutes was added to the working day, presumably, time to wash or change. However, management appropriated these 12 minutes, the power was not turned off until 5.12 and no one was allowed to leave, even one minute before that time.

At quitting time, glad to get out, I ran to catch the Spadina street car. I had forgotten all about the things growing in the springtime in the gardens of Roumania. I felt tired, hungry, disappointed and afraid.

However, I returned to work the next morning and punched in promptly in the newly-discovered time clock at one minute to eight.

Industry had claimed me! I had no choice, everyone had to earn their keep. An unwilling victim, I worked for the paper box company at $8.00 a week for six interminable months.

* * *

In her own good time, Molly made it up to me for delivering me into the maws of industry.

It was arranged that I was to live with her and her husband in that elegant apartment on Grange Avenue for a few months. They had a spare room and I slept on a pull-out couch and helped a little with the house work.

My daily contact at work with people who spoke nothing but English had improved my command of the language in a very short time.

I began to read the newspapers. When I first started I understood about half of what I read but made rapid progress mainly due to the irresistible attraction of The Gumps, Boots And Her Buddies, Maggie and Jiggs, The Captain and The Kids, in the *Star Weekly* comic section. I read Little Benny's Note Book, followed Edgar Rice Burrowes Tarzan of the Apes avidly in the *Evening Telegram,* and studied the advertisements of what was essential and important in what was now my everyday life:

MOTHER!
WATCH YOU'R CHILD'S TONGUE.
CALIFORNIA FIG SYRUP IS A CHILDS
HARMLESS LAXATIVE.

ZAM-BUK.
ALWAYS READY TO SOOTH AND
HEAL.

The Wretched of the Earth—and Me

> WOMEN!
> AVOID OPERATIONS!
> LYDIA E. PINKHAM'S VEGETABLE
> COMPOUND!
>
> CHILDREN CRY FOR FLETCHER'S
> CASTORIA. PROMOTES CHEERFUL-
> NESS, REST, NATURAL SLEEP.
>
> PEEL OFF YEARS FROM AGING
> FACES! MERCOLIZED WAX BRINGS
> OUT THE HIDDEN BEAUTY!

I still have a scar on my leg from trying out mercolized wax on my limbs. Another source of education was the beautiful rotogravure section of the *Star Weekly*, which, on Saturdays, presented the photographs of the mighty and the beautiful people of the land and abroad:

> Miss Aileen Allan of Ottawa, daughter of Mrs. Arthur Allen and niece of Mr. G.W. Allen, chairman of the Hudson Bay Co. recently presented at court in London.
>
> Prince Francis Joseph Otto, eldest son of Ex-Empress Zita of Austria is 14 years of age...(In 1989 Otto Von Hapsburg, now an old man who had spent his life in exile, turned up in Budapest as the Communist political hold was dissolving. Some opposition parties suggested Otto might run for President of Hungary....)

Upstairs, in the same apartments, lived a dressmaker, a Mrs. Cronenberg whose son, Milton, was an attractive 14-year-old on whom I looked with some favor. Milton, alas, did not return my interest. He was, somewhat later, to enrich Canadian life by becoming the father one of its most famous film producers, David Cronenberg.

One day, Molly brought home Mr. Brown, her English night-school teacher. He tutored me for $2.00 a lesson, which I paid for out of my weekly earnings of $7.00 a week; and by Christmas of that year, grateful and happy, I entered grade eight in Clinton Street public school.

Luckily I was in the very class of which Mr. Brown was form teacher.

My Toronto

Harbord St. Collegiate, Toronto, c. 1920

I have always been grateful to Molly for integrating me into the Canadian school system.

What a wonderful system! Every few hours a new teacher came and spread out before our eyes such riches as geography, grammar, arithmetic, literature and English and Canadian history. Once a week we were taken for music appreciation in a special room where records were played for us. We were introduced to *March Slav* and *In A Persian Garden*. Unforgettable! I drank it all in from the photographs of Queen Mary and King George V on the wall to the Scottish accent of the history teacher, a Mr. Wilkie. All new, all wonderful! How great not to be in that polluted, noisy hell of a paper-box factory!

At recess I kept to myself. After all, I spoke with a foreign accent, I was a 'greenie.' Will the children make fun of me? The children, however, were less prejudiced than many adults, and before long, cautious, amicable advances were made.

My new friends introduced me to the little store on Manning Avenue where one cent bought a licorice whip, chewing gum, or jelly beans. And then there were the 'grab bags.' For one penny, also, you bought a little brown bag which disclosed its delicious surprises on your eager opening; sour balls, bannana shaped and flavored candies, perhaps even a 'sucker.'

The Wretched of the Earth—and Me

The first month in a class of 40, my standing was 38. The second month I stood third and bowed my head shyly as the class applauded when the results were read out.

I really didn't have much trouble after that with being a 'greenie.' My success in school gave me backbone and confidence.

At the end of the year I was 'recommended' to enter high school, which meant that I didn't have to write entrance examinations and in the fall moved back to sister Rosie's house on Major Street to enter one of the best High Schools in the city, Harbord Collegiate.

I didn't know the meaning of 'swot' and that among students it was to go in and out of style, but I actually loved the academic work and every month I stood first which gave me much needed self-confidence. Quite as important, perhaps, I acquired two girl friends, Anne Kohen and Shirley Etlin, a friendship which enriched my life for years to come.

It was at Harbord Collegiate as well that I underwent a second name change.

"Minnie" said Colonel Haggerty the principal, "is not a real name. It's a diminutive! What is your real name? They call you 'Min?' Well, it must be short for 'Minerva.'" So I became "Minerva" at times.

My academic cleverness, during the course of one year, however, did not entitle or help me to continue school. When vacations began I was back on the labor market, unemployed.

Sweet Marie or *Turkish Delight?*

"Hello! Are you working?"

This is the customary greeting of people meeting on the avenue in the early '20s.

"How are you?" might merely inquire about one's health, whereas the first question dealt with matters of life and death—such as how to pay the weekly room and board.

We in the working-class areas lived by the Protestant principle that work is good for without work we starved. Wages were low and there was no surplus. Many a mother and father could not support a teenage child at school, nor could a working sister or brother render any assistance.

It was for such reasons that in 1922 I left the flat of my sister Rosie— her husband had demurred at having another mouth to feed—and went to live with my mother and stepfather.

He repaired shoes for a living. This trade had enabled him to bring up a family and even buy a little home on Palmerston Avenue, but there was no surplus for those wanting the luxury of going to high school instead of going to work.

Being out of work was a calamity and if we lost a job because we were laid off or, most dreaded of all, fired we immediately took steps to remedy this state of idleness by canvassing the likely factories, one after the other, and asking for employment.

I, too, set out to look for work the usual way, which was to beat the woods for where jobs might be hiding. My favorite hunting ground was the light industry area bounded by Bathurst Street in the west, Spadina Avenue in the east, Dundas Street in the north and Wellington Street in the south.

At first I was somewhat embarrassed.

"Are there any jobs?"

Was that something like asking for a handout? However, I discovered

The Wretched of the Earth—and Me

to my relief that it is usual office routine to attend to the counter where people might come asking for work and I was even invited to fill out an application once, which was very encouraging.

I would set myself goals in this hunt.

"I'll do Adelaide Street, this afternoon," I said to my mother, "And Spadina on the way back." I walked both ways, of course. A streetcar ticket was 7 cents, 15 cents return—a lot of money. Occasionally, I spent 5 cents for a cup of coffee, but not very often.

A car ticket at 7 cents might have seemed like a great deal of money to an unemployed girl but even so the public transport system was a blessing to the people of Toronto. There were automobiles, but we all travelled by streetcar when we could afford it.

Public transportation in Toronto—there were only streetcars—was very efficient and cheap. The fare was 5 cents for a long time, until it was raised to 7 cents. Young men took their girls out on dates by streetcar, which had leather straps to hang on to if all the seats were taken. The streetcars were heated in winter by a coal stove that the conductor had to stoke and look after. Young men, gentlemen all, offered ladies their seats, even during rush hour.

At the end of an afternoon of tramping around in the snow in my sloppy galloshes—which were not snowproof, of course—I would sit in our large kitchen by my mother's wood-burning stove, eat an apple and read a book, tired but not discouraged.

My mother's stove—it burned wood and coal—was the true family hearth. It was the centre of comfort and entertainment in the winter, featured a warming closet and heated water in its boiler, which held four–and–a–half Imperial gallons. This stove, which was always going in cold weather, made the large kitchen the coziest room in the house. Often there was a pot of soup simmering at the back and for our dinner mother cooked the most wonderful dishes. Because they were slow cooked, she could use the toughest and therefore the cheapest cuts of meat.

Coffee cakes, *strudel, mandelbrot* (almondbread) and *lekach* (traditional honey cake) would issue from that oven on Fridays to perfume the kitchen with a delicious odor. We also made toast by lifting up one of the plates covering a cooking hole with a tool provided for that purpose and extending a slice over the coal-fire with a long-handled fork; we watched the bread toast to perfection.

I was never prodded into going out job hunting, nor were there inquiries as to whether I had been successful in my search.

Sweet Marie or Turkish Delight?

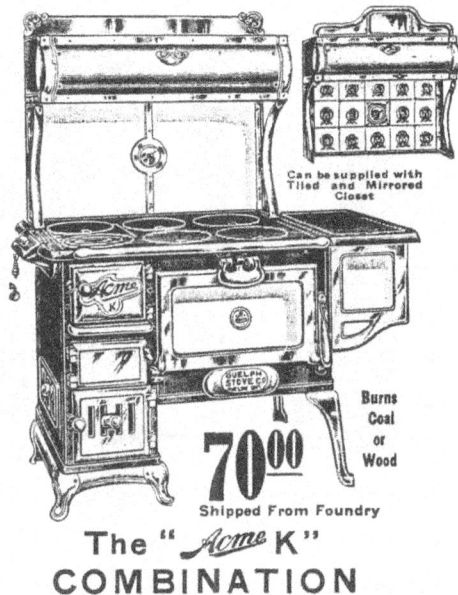

My mother's coal and wood burning stove.

Coal & wood burning stove, c. 1920

It was understood that if I found work, I would announce the good news. Nevertheless, aware that I was not contributing to household expenses, I felt guilty.

Everyone was sympathetic to my troubles and I was released from certain household tasks that usually fell to Anne and me to carry out. For instance, we had lace panels on all the windows. These were bought from Eaton's catalogue at $1.65 a pair and they were forever being taken down, washed, mended and hung up again. Anne did the curtains without asking me to do my share.

"You forgot, it's your turn," Anne would remind me on Sundays about the washing of our linoleum-covered floors. This 'oilcloth' was cracked with age and I used to toil away at it to bring back the pretty pattern, which had been worn off by foot traffic. I was relieved of this job, too, when unemployed.

But I was not excused from laundry duty. Laundry day was very important, and since Anne was working I had to help mother with this arduous task, which began the evening before with the soaking of the clothes overnight.

The Wretched of the Earth—and Me

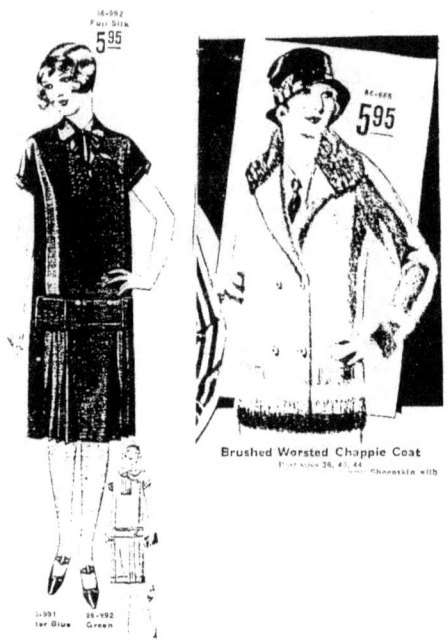

Girl's outfit, Toronto, c. 1920

Early in the morning, washing commenced in a tub placed on two chairs in the kitchen, then a great deal of scrubbing went on by means of a washboard. Finally the clothes were boiled on the stove in another tub.

We hung our washing out in the sun in the summer and let the frost get at it in the winter, which kept our linen sparkling white. There was a struggle during cold weather to bring in sheets that were frozen to the line in the backyard and stiff as boards, in addition.

After laundry day I was almost glad to get back to job hunting.

Sometimes, amazingly enough, I was actually hired. The jobs I found were of short duration and it seemed that very often, one of the contracting parties wanted out quite soon after employment commenced.

It was in this haphazard manner that I was sporadically successful in helping light industry supply its eager customers with the products of my labor in Christmas seals, butterscotch candy, cards of safety pins and 'suit backs, ladies' from which the bastings had been pulled out by me for one whole afternoon of employment.

I had trouble with industry and industry had trouble with me!

"You are fired," they said to me after I had counted Christmas seals for two whole weeks.

Sweet Marie or Turkish Delight?

I rather liked this publishing-printing-bookbinding plant on Wellington Street, where all I had to do was count off 50 Christmas seals and tags and place them in a transparent envelope that would eventually be sold for 10 cents. The work was clean, the time passed quickly and there were other girls of my age.

However, I had a great deal more initiative than the job called for. I decided on the third day that 55 and sometimes 60 seals instead of 50 would prove a pleasant surprise for customers at Christmas time. It was an unpleasant surprise for me when I was unceremoniously dismissed for my largesse. Dismissal was instantaneous. The foreman simply went into the office, had my pay made up and handed me the little brown envelope. I had to leave immediately.

The Scottish forelady at the famous butterscotch plant—they showed a lot of Tartan in their advertisements—on Wolseley Street was decidedly cool to me when she found out I was Jewish. It was not difficult to find my work unsatisfactory and once more I suffered the dire fate of being fired.

I went in and out of the clothing trades on Spadina Avenue, all in one afternoon. I wasn't fast enough at pulling the bastings out from the 'ladies backs' and I didn't much care for the handsome foreman who sent around a free Coca Cola and wanted me to stay after 5 o'clock so he could teach me the work.

The reward for these jobs hovered around $7 a week.

One day, searching again on Wellington Street, I was astounded when in answer to my usual query of "Are there any jobs?" the clerk said: "Wait a minute."

The foreman actually offered me employment, at $9 a week, in his large and well-known chocolate factory, which was the birthplace and the cradle of my favorite *Sweet Marie* candy bar.

I was to sit at a machine and mind the variously-shaped items which came along a moving belt to be covered with chocolate at a certain point. My task was to separate with my finger any bars which might adhere to each other through the action of the hot chocolate which was gently spraying down in liquid form a meter away.

I suffered much love and much hate in that chocolate factory.

Here I was, still possessed by my insatiable appetite for sweets, surrounded by Canada's greatest variety of chocolate bars and all for free.

On this belt came along in oblong, square and round form, crisp

The Wretched of the Earth—and Me

cherries enveloped in a sherbert-like cream, roasted peanuts bedded down on chewy honey-blond toffee, rich shredded coconut immersed in thick, sweet condensed milk and reminiscent of the delicacies brought by sister Dora to Roumania, graceful layers of crunchy wafer bonded with fragrant creams, even *Turkish Delight* squares arrived to be covered with chocolate and to move slowly past, until, by the time they reached a receptacle at the end of the belt, the chocolate was dry and ready for me to eat.

On the first day I consumed so much chocolate I did not touch my dinner. However, I continued to eat the sweets, in diminishing quantities, for many days to come.

After about two weeks I noticed with distaste, that my clothes carried the odour of chocolate, and even my coat, hung up in the cloak room emitted that unpleasant scent.

We had no clothes cupboards as such in our home. Everyone used the one walnut wardrobe with the two mirrored doors which was, conveniently for us, placed in our bedroom. Winter coats were hung up in an area in the entrance to the cellar. There was no way I could keep my clothes away from those of the family. I knew that the odour of chocolate was very strong and pervasive. I could even tell which were my workmates as they walked on Wellington Street by the smell their clothes wafted about in the air.

I was perishing with embarrassment! Could the people on the street car tell by their noses that I was a chocolate factory worker?

I had read Bizet's opera *Carmen* (part of my educational reading in Roumania) and I knew all about cigarette factory girls. Were chocolate shop girls regarded as of easy virtue as well?

Dora's *scandale* had imbued all of her sisters, particularly me, with the fear of being regarded as 'easy' and with considering flirtatiousness as immoral. I never looked at a man, was not pleasant to them and responded rudely to any approach. I despised the joshing and kidding going on among my fellow workers and walked with my head down on the street. Besides, I was interested in other matters, for I was still hot in quest of books, education and anything to do with what I regarded as intellectual pursuits.

Because of the chocolate smell, I had to have more clothes. I went window shopping. Usually, we bought a dress a season. Summer dresses were being shown but they were cheaper from the catalogue. A two-

Sweet Marie or Turkish Delight?

Ladies' outfits c. 1920

The Wretched of the Earth—and Me

piece cotton pongee dress was $2.50, a Fuji Silk was $5.95, but I should save for the stylish wool cardigan—a (Chappie coat they called it) expensive at $5.95—and there were 'balbriggan bloomers' I needed too; they were 40 cents a pair.

However, after the room and board apportionment there was not much left for clothes, so it was just as well that mother insisted on a never-to-be–departed– from discipline of doing our own washing and cleaning.

Every Sunday we polished our shoes, washed our underwear, stockings and blouses and cleaned our non-washable garments. By means of a wet cloth and a hot iron we took creases out and refreshed clothing we would need for the week's wear. The iron was of metal, sometimes called a 'sad iron.' It was heated on the stove and used quickly, before it got cold. Very infrequently, a Chinese laundry was employed but for a special occasion only. A shirt cost 10 cents for laundering. It was delivered by the Chinese laundryman and if he was used on several occasions during the year, at Christmas he arrived with a bag of Lichee nuts for a present.

Our hosiery were cotton stockings and they lasted a long time. Holes and runs were carefully mended.

Apparently, mens' clothing was more expensive. Frank's Clothing Wear at 368 Queen St. E. was advertising:

SUITS,
CLEARING AT
$12.95 (REG. $37.50)

I settled the problem of additional clothing by buying a 'middy' blouse with a braid-trimmed collar and a slip-through tie for $1.19.

As for my chocolate eating, before long, my appetite for sweets declined and then disappeared altogether.

I was left with the problem of life on the belt line where the hours dragged along at a pace set by the slow-moving chocolate bars.

Time, was watching the movement of a never-ending array of brown objects barely creeping past, hour after hour, week after week.

It was destroying my mind. I tried reciting poetry, rehearsing things I had learned. It was useless. My mind searched vainly for something with which to occupy itself, something on which to chew. If I could only read a book!

I learned in later years that the workers who made hand-rolled cigars, Spanish mostly, to escape the monotony of their work, paid people to

Sweet Marie or Turkish Delight?

read to them while they worked. The type of literature read was of a high caliber: Gorky, Hugo, Tolstoy were favorites. Poetry was read out loud.

I, however, suffered unending agony attending the belt. Each minute stretched into an hour, each hour into a day.

"What am I doing here?" I said to myself. "And why?"

My rational mind resented having to become an appendage to this loathsome machine and to become involved in its brown, gooey objectives.

To confirm my fantasy that I was an adjunct of the machine, three young men arrived one day with a stop watch. The belt was accelerated, the belt was slowed down; there was much timing and counting. No one asked me how the various speeds affected my functioning, whether I could cope, whether I was more comfortable sitting or standing up. In fact, they didn't even glance at me. I wanted to shout "Hey fellows, look at me, I'm human, I count too."

The time-and-motion-study men had slighted me as a woman and as a human being but I felt a different sort of indignation as well. I resented their presence for I knew they were there for the other side, for the owners, the bosses. My class-consciousness was growing, nourished by the fetid climate of a factory system to which I could not adjust.

For eight hours every day I struggled against the dormant effect of the belt line; only when I came home did I become alive and happy again.

Not too happy, however. I was thwarted, frustrated on many levels.

It was 1927. I had only been in Canada for 8 years and I was very self-conscious still about being, what was called on the street, a 'greenie.' To my mortification my English still betrayed more than traces of a foreign accent which caused me continual anguish. I was devoured by the need to immerse myself in Canadianism and wash off the stain of being an 'alien.' I felt the rejection all around me.

The native Torontonians, presumably all white, Anglo Saxons and Protestants (WASP!) looked down on and despised all newcomers giving them the hardest work to do and the least pay. 'Aliens,' 'bohunks,' 'greenies' were everyday expressions.

"Why don't you go back where you came from?" was the ultimate insult. Perhaps it started on the wake of the Winnipeg General Strike in 1919 when the non-Anglo Saxons were villified in the WASP press:

The Wretched of the Earth—and Me

> Enemy aliens have taken an active part in every disturbance that has occurred In Winnipeg. It is time the authorities rounded up every man of alien blood who cannot show himself worthy of citizenship and send him back to the hovel from which he sprang.
>
> *Daily News Chronicle* Port Arthur, June 13, 1919.

(See *The Ukrainians in Winnipeg's First Century* by Peter Krawchuk).

Toronto, cemented in conservatism, was all for King and Country, the Flag and the Orange Lodge. I sensed a little of this and was longing to be accepted by the King and the country and the Orange Lodge. I was particularly attracted to the Orange Lodge. When July 12th came around (my birthday), I watched with envy, enthusiasm and affection the huge parade, led by fife and drum bands whose practicing could be heard around town, weeks before the event.

The Orange Lodge paraded so magnificently!

There were dignitaries on horses. there were lovely silk banners held high by members of various lodges, there were gentlemen in top hats who were bedecked with wide, over-the-shoulder red satin sashes and the Ladies Auxiliaries in their beautiful white dresses with wide orange silk bands encircling their waists, carried banners proudly proclaiming that they belonged to this important and powerful native Canadian Society. How I longed to belong to the Orange Lodge!

It was all very frustrating!

My friends, Anne Kohn and Shirley Etlin were still attending high school, feeding their intellect, while I trudged daily to my factory job.

The fertile mind, however, casts about for remedies for its own unhappy state. One day, I read an advertisement in the papers which stated that "Dominion Business College, upstairs on Bloor Street can train girls to be secretaries in three months. Night courses are available." I eagerly enrolled.

I pursued the business course with a passion fed by my hatred of those brown chocolate bars filing by on the belt.

I rented a typewriter. I practiced 'Pittman's shorthand.' I never missed an hour of night school. Financially it was difficult. Out of my $9.00 a week earnings, $5.00 went for room and board (every decent child in

Sweet Marie or Turkish Delight?

Richmond St. Toronto, c. 1925

Toronto paid room and board when working; families depended on it), $3.00 went for school fees at the business college and $1.00 was left over for carfare. Mother always made my lunches.

In three months' time I graduated from the business college and, better still, in a brief five days I had obtained a job as a junior stenographer for a leather goods manufacturer on Richmond Street.

From Richmond and Duncan Streets I walked home that day, to Palmerston Avenue and Dundas on rosy clouds of joy and achievement. My mother cried when I told her the good news and we had tea with apple strudel.

The Study Circle

At home on Palmerston Avenue, since everyone was working, peace and contentment reigned. But one day I came home to great excitement.

"Come upstairs to the bathroom and see," said Anne.

The hated small bathroom—unbearably hot in the summer and painfully cold in the winter—housed mine enemy: a tin bathtub that resisted all my scrubbing, making it barely acceptable to bathe in and quick to get darkly tarnished right after use. (I had an idea that if one rubbed and polished long enough, it would get bright and shiny like the copper pans we had in Roumania, but it never did.)

And here it was now, replaced by a beautiful white enamel tub fitted with water connections, 'waste and overflow,' as the accompanying brochure from Eaton's Catalogue Spring and Summer 1927, said. (Such things are cheaper when ordered from the catalogue.)

The bathtub augmented our household conveniences, which were not very extensive. There was no living room and no upholstered furniture. We had a front room, however, which boasted a 'dining set,' used once a year at Passover time for the *seder* (the Passover dinner during which the exodus of the Jews from Egypt is retold.)

The greatest discomfort we suffered had to do with heating.

For that purpose, a 'self-heater' existed—called a 'selafeater'—which was a coal-fed, round stove located in the middle of the downstairs hall. Black tin pipes carried the heat to the upstairs rooms. Either they didn't transport the heat very well or there wasn't much heat. At any rate, the upstairs where we slept at first, was always frightfully cold in the winter. It wasn't much warmer downstairs.

Still, we were blessed with electricity—but no appliances.

Mother had an old Singer sewing machine that she treasured and at which she spent many hours pushing away at the treadle, sewing curtains for the house and aprons and slips for herself and the girls.

In summertime, life was truly easy. Our 'yard' was grass-covered and contained beautiful things—rambler roses climbing up the wall of the parents' bedroom and a cherry tree that rained down pink blossoms in the spring and produced many pounds of good eating cherries. We had an icebox and bought ice three times a week—some people bought ice only for the weekends—and we could keep some foodstuffs cool in the cellar. In an emergency, butter and milk were stored in a pan of cold water in the sink.

In the wintertime we placed our milk and butter on the windowsills. One neighbor had a 'summer pantry'—actually a little unheated room next to the kitchen that had many good uses.

Mother shopped daily, of course, and bought just 5 cents' worth of this and 15 cents' worth of that, so there was not much need for food storage. In the Jewish butcher shop, flank steak was 15 cents a pound. A. & P. advertised sirloin steak at 35 cents a pound, while Arnold Meat Market had veal at 25 cents a pound. Two half-pound tins of salmon cost 34 cents and fresh Restigouche salmon was only 33 cents a pound. Back bacon was the same price, not that there was any of *that* in our house.

There were no supermarkets in our neighborhood. Mother had her favorite grocery store on Dundas Street, owned by a Mrs. Mirvish. I went in sometimes and was waited on by her very polite, good-looking son, Eddie, who moved from Dundas Street only as far as Bloor and Markham Street to set himself up as "Honest Ed" not many years later.

We did not rely entirely on the stores for our provisions. On Fridays mother baked her own bread—the egg-bread called *challah*—and delicious coffee cakes and strudel. The strudel was the French pastry type; Mama would stretch the pastry until it was paper-thin and covering the whole kitchen table, then fill it with apple and walnuts, or sweetened cottage cheese, or minced meat, or, best of all, Turkish Delight and toasted filberts.

In the autumn, a barrel of red peppers that we stuffed with sliced cabbage was put down besides the jars of gherkins and green tomatoes for the winter, everything being well doused with garlic and dill.

There were surprises from time to time, as on one June day when sister Anne hailed me on my return from work. She was very excited.

"Come in the kitchen, Minnie, and see—quick!"

Spread out on the kitchen table on a white cloth was a mass of pink rose petals, perfuming the air. I knew immediately what it was.

"Oh, I know. We are going to make rose jam."

A neighbor had allowed Anne to pick about 120 fat, huge cabbage

The Wretched of the Earth and—Me

Shea's, Toronto, c. 1925

roses. It was easy! Just as we did in Roumania, we sprinkled the petals with lemon juice to retain the color, then added sugar and cooked the mixture quickly. It boiled down considerably, but we ended up with five priceless little jars.

When opened in December, at *Chanukah* time, the jam brought the precious fragrance of June roses into the house.

Anne and I became chummy again and we went out together on Saturday afternoons. As purveyors of art and culture, we were more than willing to try the movies and shows.

Shea's, The Home of Keith's Super Vaudeville advertised 1,000 matinee seats daily for 25 cents.

The beautiful *Tivoli* at Richmond and Victoria Streets presented *Souls For Sables*, with Eugene O'Brien and Claire Windsor. Music was provided by Louigi Romanelli and "His King Edward Syncopators." The price was 25 cents in the afternoon and 50 cents in the evening.

Anne and I made sure we didn't miss *The Fool*, with Edmund Lowe.

And there was no moral taint attached to attending burlesque shows.

Abbot's Strand on Yonge Street near King featured "Burlesque As It Should Be—20 Charming Town Rounders 20" and we went to see them.

My mother and stepfather had their own amusements. On Saturday they used to walk from Dundas and Palmerston to Eaton's, which was at Queen and Yonge, a good mile and more.

"Well, what did you buy today?" I would ask them on their return, knowing full-well they had bought nothing. The trip was purely for entertainment and to console themselves for not having any spare money to spend, they pronounced everything was *chozerei* (junk). Sometimes, they would produce a 15-cent bag of chocolate 'maple buds' or peanut-butter filled *satinettes*, or Turkish Delight for the next strudel.

As young teenagers, our amusements were equally simple. "Going to the library" was a weekly entertainment and I would come back from the library at St. George and College Streets with my arms loaded with books.

As I was slowly working my way through James Oliver Curwood, Marie Corelli, Zane Grey and Victor Hugo—and through luck or good sense avoiding the popular Ethel M. Dell—I made a great discovery. At last! A novelist who was critical of our society and presented an alternate system—in the future. I feverishly devoured every one of the books of H.G. Wells and looked around for others, but found none.

Anne was not quite so interested in reading but in the summertime we would take the streetcar to the end of the line, usually to Main and Danforth Avenue, and then walk in the open fields and meadows or take the "RADIAL," an inter-urban transport system, to "the country"—Richmond Hill.

If we had had the money, we could have gone on a 16-day seashore excursion to Atlantic City for $16.80 return. And if we had had even more, we could have bought property cheaply:

FOR SALE
OWNER'S HOME
CHAPLIN BETWEEN YONGE AND ORIOLE PARKWAY
$10,500.00

A.E. LePage advertised:

MANSION FOR SALE FOR A SONG

The Wretched of the Earth and—Me

> SOUTH ROSEDALE, OWNER'S HOME. 12 ROOMS, 4
> BATHROOMS, BILLIARD ROOM, 3-CAR GARAGE WITH
> CHAUFFER'S QUARTERS, $30,000

In the late 1920s, the coming Depression cast its long shadows ahead and jobs went from hard-to-get to non-existent. Employment Wanted classified ads in the *Toronto Star* cost 1 cent a word, cash, with a 15-cent minimum.

Not many jobs were advertised.

On July 3, 1928, there were 21 ads from employers looking for me, including:

> TEN MEN FOR MARKET GARDEN,
> TWO TALL BOYS FOR FRUIT
> PICKING

and

> MESSENGER BOY WANTED,
> DAY OR NIGHT, MCLEAN'S DRUG STORE,
> MADISON AND DUPONT ST.

There were equally few jobs in the "Help Wanted, Female" column.

Women who had to earn a living found life hard. Some were pushed into criminal activities. They shoplifted, they forged checks, they drank. The best the city could do was to provide them with a Women's Police Court, presided over by a female magistrate—Magistrate Patterson, in 1928. This we found out when a friend of Anne's was arrested for shoplifting.

Out of work, broke and wandering around Eaton's for something to do, she picked up a slip and stuffed it into her pocket.

"I didn't know there would be detectives dressed like plain people," she complained.

Magistrate Patterson dealt gently with her. She suspended sentence, and warned her to keep out of the store. Others were not so lucky. "Florence" pleaded guilty on that day to being intoxicated. Her first offence, she was given the option of "$10 or 10 days." "Mary Woods" was fined $10 and given the option of 30 days in jail for trespassing. "Lucille" appeared on eight charges of fraud, forgery and putting false

The Study Circle

Eaton's., Toronto, c. 1925

checks into circulation. She was released on $2,000 bail, this being a more important crime and requiring representation by counsel.

Now that I worked in an office, I didn't find life too hard except that I chafed at not being able to fit into the life of the community.

Nor did I feel more at ease in my own age group. When, finally, through some miracle, I got invited to 'a party with boys,' I was a failure there, as well. I never said anything amusing, I couldn't giggle, I stepped on the boys' feet when dancing and I thought the 'shimmy' vulgar. The girls were interested in clothes and in making themselves ever more attractive.

"I love red," said Darkhead to me at a party as she tied a scarlet scarf straight across her forehead. I was appalled at my own lack of interest in such things.

"Three boys have already asked me out for next week," said Red Kerchief triumphantly. "You got a date yet?" She knew well enough I didn't have a date, nor was I asked to another party.

Fortunately, I had two devoted girl friends, Anne and Shirley, and despite our collective good luck, we languished in our unpopularity together. We tried hard to amuse ourselves.

The Wretched of the Earth and—Me

Royal Ontario Museum, Toronto, c. 1925

Sundays, particularly in the winter, were desperately dull and boring as there was nowhere to go, movies were forbidden on the Sabbath day and we knew every corner of the Royal Ontario Museum.

One day, a friend of Anne's asked: "Would you and your friends like to come to a little 'reading circle' that meets on Sunday nights?"

Would we? We were grateful, for Toronto at the time was deep in the grip of Sunday 'blue laws' and everything was shut up tight except the churches. Toronto's important citizens, mostly from the British Isles, were largely Presbyterian, Methodist or United Church. Very pious, conventionally religious, they were; in addition more patriotic about the old country and the Royal Family than the British would ever have considered necessary or even good form. They equated patriotism with religion and insisted that Sunday be kept by every citizen of Toronto strictly for going to church.

Representing such an electorate, the city fathers in their political wisdom decreed, for one decade after the other, that on Sundays every activity must cease except walking and that, preferably, to church. The corner tobacco store was closed; movies, concerts, plays and all forms of

The Study Circle

Victor Himmelfarb, c. 1925

sports were outlawed; and hockey, even when played by small boys on the corner lot or rink, was forbidden.

We jumped eagerly at Diana Shiner's invitation.

All week I anticipated the event and finally the day arrived. It is wet, cold and sad, a typical Toronto Sunday evening in February.

Dressed in our weekend best we are there, ringing the door bell shortly after 8 o'clock. It is very quiet, there is no sound of merriment or even of voices. Maybe we have the wrong address? But someone opens the door and we go in.

Sitting around in an actual circle, young men and some young women, about twenty-five in all, look up with interest at the three pretty girls entering the room. They are taking turns reading aloud a paragraph or two at a time out of a slim yellow booklet.

Like a stage setting prepared for presentation of Act I, Scene I, they are offering *The Manifesto Of The Communist Party*, by Karl Marx and Frederick Engels. We are seated and invited to participate.

Sharing the brochure with Victor Himmelfarb, a founding member of the Young Communist League (YCL), I hear the ringing words:

The Wretched of the Earth and—Me

> "The history of all hitherto existing society is the history of class struggles.
>
> "Freeman and slave, patrician and plebeian, lord and serf, guild-master and journeyman, in a word oppressor and oppressed, stood in constant opposition to one another, carried on an uninterrupted now hidden, now open fight, a fight that each time ended either in a revolutionary re-constitution of society at large or in the common ruin of the contending classes......
>
> "Our epoch, the epoch of the bourgeoisie, possesses however this distinctive feature: it has simplified the class antagonisms. Society as a whole, is more and more splitting up into great classes directly facing each other: Bourgeoisie and Proletariat..."

We read on and I listen astounded. This is it! Revelation! Not the blinding light that comes to the seekers of religious truth but one of a more momentous kind, a sociological revelation. So this is what is wrong with society, this is the answer I am searching for. This small group, led by the book they are reading, has the answers to all the questions I've been asking. Here is an explanation of the basic flaws of our society, the means by which society could be changed, a cause and an instrument dedicated to effecting this change. How wonderful!

We went home, atwitter with the excitement of it all.

An overwhelming flood of new ides and concepts followed particularly at the meeting of the English branch (I was to learn there were also Jewish and Ukrainian branches) of the Young Communist League to which we were all invited.

Here we met a group of brilliant young men—Oscar Ryan, who was national secretary of the Young Communist League (a full-time job); Charlie Marriott, its leading literary light; Leslie Morris, a romantic figure of Welsh descent and Ukrainian inclination, and Stewart Smith, very blond, very good looking and surrounded by the aura of having just returned from the Lenin Institute—a sort of a Communist university. (Actually, it was openly run by the Communist International as a school for the training of Communist leaders and the only secrecy connected with it was the necessity of protecting the identity of students who came

The Study Circle

Charlie Marriot, c. 1919

from such countries as Italy, Hungary and Germany, where membership alone in the Communist movement could spell imprisonment, torture and death. Terrorism was not on the curriculum nor approved of as a method of advancing the class struggle; (see, *Which Side Are You on Boys?* by Peter Hunter.)

Everything was impressive to me in my naivete.

First of all, there was an Agenda for the meeting. I knew nothing of Agendas; in fact, it is the first time I ever heard the word and I was properly impressed by its divisions into Minutes of the Last Meeting, New Business Arising from the Last Item, and I especially loved, Good and Welfare. For years afterwards I had to restrain myself from finding things to bring up under Good and Welfare, just because it was there.

And then they asked, "Can I have the floor?" ("Sure, have it," I said to myself with idiotic glee. "But how are you going to pick it up?") People made Motions that had to have Seconders and at the end there even had to be a Motion to Adjourn, which had to be Carried Unanimously. Otherwise, I supposed, we could not go home, ever.

The members called each other Comrade, which sounded strange and

The Wretched of the Earth and—Me

embarrassing at first. (However, calling someone Comrade did not prevent them from attacking that very same person verbally and in a very non-comradely fashion.)

There were reports from higher bodies such as the District Executive Committee (DEC) and even from a Provincial Committee.

People were being nominated and elected in very rapid order to all sorts of committees. There was a heady moment when I was elected editor of the *Wall Newspaper*. While I was still savouring the moment, there was a motion, carried unanimously, to adjourn the meeting and we sang *The Internationale*, calling on the wretched of the earth to arise, assuring them that a better world was in birth:

> *Arise ye prisoners of starvation*
> *Arise ye wretched of the earth*
> *For Justice thunders condemnation*
> *A better world's in birth*
> *No more tradition's chains shall bind us,*
> *Arise ye slaves no more in thrall,*
> *The earth shall rise on new foundations*
> *We have been naught, we shall be all.*

It was all very thrilling and inspiring and uplifting and I wanted more, more of this new world in birth.

We continued to attend the Study Circle on Sundays and I found ever more intellectual satisfaction in the Marxist explanations of the workings of the capitalist system and its fatal flaws.

The names of the little booklets that carried this precious information were honey in my mouth and its tones were sweet to my ears—*Value, Price And Profit, Wage-Labour And Capital* and *Socialism, Utopian and Scientific*. It is true that about a year later I had trouble with *The Peasant Question In France And Germany*, written by Frederick Engels in 1894 and no matter how hard and dutifully I tried, I failed to find any lessons in it for Canada. We were always finding lessons in this or that historical happening, and lucky was the comrade who had to write an article and was able to pepper it with apt quotations from Marx, Lenin and, later, Stalin. I ousted my nagging doubts and disloyal thoughts by assuring myself that other comrades who know more about the farmers out west could probably see the connection.

(Oddly enough, Engels was right; the small farms in Canada were displaced by larger farms, a continuing process.)

The Study Circle

There were many aspects of the movement to be explored.

I was fascinated by the comrades from the Jewish Branch, with their literary Yiddish, their knowledge of Jewish writers and poets and their preoccupation with the mandolin orchestra, the folk choir and other Jewish cultural activities. In the summer time, at Camp *Naivelt* (New World) there was a *cultur vinkl* (culture nook) under a tree where every afternoon the works of Sholem Aleichem and other Jewish writers were read aloud.

At 300 Bathurst Street, there were Ukrainian comrades to be visited, for this was the Toronto headquarters of the Ukrainian Farmer-Labor Temple Association (ULFTA). Here, too, were groups playing the mandolin and practising magnificent Ukrainian dancing. A choir of mixed voice sang at concerts and festivals.

At the Don Hall, 957 Broadview Avenue, Finnish comrades continually staged plays—in Finnish only, alas! Still, they were fun to watch and excellent coffee and a special type of coffee cake was sold very cheaply.

I caught glimpses of many fascinating people; they were all my comrades and suddenly I felt I belonged. I was accepted as an equal, my abilities, such as they were, were being used. I was happy with my new friends and completely prepared to devote myself wholly and gratefully to the cause.

There was a bible, I discovered, for the new creed.

It was Upton Sinclair's anthology, *The Cry For Justice,* and I revelled in each story, poem and extract that mirrored my feelings and hopes.

I plunged right in and adopted everything, walking around with a self-satisfied look, my head no longer bent to the ground.

"You look like you just discovered *America* all over again," said my mother, who noticed everything about her children.

I had, and was busy memorizing my self-chosen catechism, "The Revolutionist" from a section of *Cry For Justice* designated as "Martyrdom." I liked that! It is about a Russian maid becoming a revolutionary and it is cruelly specific and heroic on a grand scale:

> *I saw a spacious house. O'erhung with pall,*
> *A narrow doorway pierced the sombre wall.*
> *Within was chill, impenetrable shade;*

The Wretched of the Earth and—Me

Without there stood a maid—a Russian maid,
To whom the icy dark sent forth a slow
And hollow sounding Voice:

"And dost thou know,
When thou hast entered, what awaits thee here?"
" I know," she said, "and knowing do not fear."
"Cold, hunger, hatred, Slander's blighting breath,"
The Voice still chanted, "suffering—and Death?"
" I know," she said.

"Undaunted, wilt thou dare
The sneers of kindred? Art thou steeled to bear
From those whom most thou lovest, spite and scorn?"
"Though love be paid with Hate, that shall be borne."
"Think! Thy doom may be to die
By thine own hand, with none to fathom why,
Unthanked, unhonored, desolate, alone,
Thy grave unmarked, thy toil, thy love unknown,
And none in days to come shall speak thy name."
She said: "I ask no pity, thanks or fame."
"Art thou prepared for crime?"

She bowed her head:
"Yes, crime, if that shall need," the maiden said.
Now paused the Voice before it asked anew:
"But knowest thou that all that holdest true
Thy soul may yet deny in bitter pain,
So thou shalt deem thy sacrifice in vain?"
"E'en this I know," she said, "and yet again
I pray thee, let me enter."
"Enter then!" That hollow Voice replied.
She passed the door
A sable curtain fell—and nothing more.
"A fool" snarled some one, gnashing. Like a prayer
"A saint!" the whispered answer thrilled the air.

—Ivan Turgenev

(Turgenev, 1818-1883, was a Russian writer, one of the masters of the

The Study Circle

novel form. He was imprisoned and later exiled. The original, the present extract is a prose-poem; versification is by Arthur Guiterman.)

* * *

It is the first of May, 1927—MAY DAY. A meeting to celebrate the workingmen's holiday is being held at Queen's Park. It is addressed by leaders of the Party and I return home, happy and inspired and wearing a red ribbon on my coat. My mother and Anne are appalled.

"In Roumania where we come from nice girls don't go mixing around in public with goodness knows what kind of rough men. Mrs. Shansky next door tells me you hang around with Russian *moujiks*. Her son told her. What are you doing there? You don't belong there. They are not your kind. And not even Jewish. It's not nice. What will become of you?"

Was this my beloved Mama talking like that? And to call my comrades in the ULFTA *moujiks* was unbearable. Darn that Mrs. Shansky next door!

"But Mama, they're Socialists." (Maybe she'll know about socialists.)

"Mrs. Shansky," continued Mama, "calls your friends 'the lefties.'"

"That's right, Mama," I said.

I thought perhaps if I explained something of the meaning of the word 'left' she wouldn't feel so much as though it was the equivalent of leper or, worse still, street walker.

"It comes from the Russian parliament, called the *duma*," I continued importantly. "The ones that sat on the right side were the *Menshevicks*, and those that sat on the left side of the House were called *Bolsheviks* because they sat on the left side, you see." Luckily, I had just come upon this little historical tidbit the week before, but mother waved the *Bolsheviks* and the *Mensheviks* away.

She recognized disaster when it struck the family.

Life *a la Jimmy Higgins*

Jimmy Higgins was a New York printer who gave his life for the socialist movement, immersing himself in the minutae of daily chores and dying of tuberculosis brought on by overwork. He was the Socialist Party's candidate for vice-president in the United States in 1904 and a legend in the left-wing movement.

There was no question of our hesitating even for one moment to join formally the four-year-old Young Communist League. We jumped into the new milieu, palpitating with excitement. Floating about were all sorts of honorary positions, available for the volunteering or the 'accepting' at the meetings of the English Branch.

I accepted the job of being an editor and considered starting at the top of the newspaper profession not a bit unusual.

The newspaper was a *wallpaper*, a miniature of a regular tabloid. The size of a regular newspaper page, it consisted of several sheets of foolscap, pasted together and affixed to cardboard. It hung on the wall of our meeting room at the Alhambra Hall, 450 Spadina Avenue (upstairs), a new issue coming out every time a new editor was elected—that is, not very regularly.

The editor would choose an appropriate news item to feature, involving perhaps a banner headline, and then run a few more news items. There were a satisfyingly large number of items to choose from, all originating from our own activities.

JUDGE QUASHES CONVICTION OF
BECKY BUHAY
CONVICTED OF VAGRANCY AFTER
ADDRESSING A
MEETING AT SOHO AND QUEEN.

HARVEY MURPHY
ARRESTED TRYING TO ADDRESS A
STREET MEETING.

The Study Circle

MR. JUSTICE RANEY HAS QUASHED
MAGISTRATE
COATSWORTH'S CONVICTION OF
HARVEY MURPHY
ARRESTED TRYING TO ADDRESS
A STREET CORNER MEETING.

JUDGE DENTON DECLARES NOT
SEDITIOUS LITERATURE
DISTRIBUTED BY EMILY WEIR.

C.F.C.A. (DAILY STAR)
BROADCASTS THE FIRST OF
A SERIES OF MONTHLY TEA HOURS
FEATURING
THE FAMOUS HAMBOURG TRIO,
CLEMENT HAMBOURG, PIANIST,
VINO HARISAY, VIOLINIST
AND BORIS HAMBOURG, CELLIST.

Then there was a corner for the editorial, a special interest column "what's doing in our branches," a 'human interest' story, which did not range very far afield, and that was it.

Simultaneously, I was informing myself about the Communist movement, learning the special language in which we understood one another, and reading its literature.

The 'Red Bishop,' William Montgomery Brown, had written *Banish God from the Sky and Capitalists from Earth*. I had, since age 13, when matters started developing very unsatisfactorily for me, also banished the idea of a personal god from my life and became a violent atheist. Bishop Montgomery suited me just fine and I happily ingested all of the Red Bishop's little pamphlets and went to hear his lecture at Hyegia Hall, 40 Elm Street—"Revolution and Evolution."

Other pamphlets available at that time were: *Misleaders of Labor* by Wm. Z. Foster, secretary of the Communist Party of the U.S.A. ($1.25); *Ten Years of the Communist International* by I. Kromer, (25¢); *The Revolutionary Movement in the Colonies*, (25¢); *Paris on the Barricades*, by George Spiro, (50¢) and for $1 one could get *Lenin On Organization*.

An editor had to be well-informed.

I carefully studied the *Young Worker*, the organ of the Young

The Wretched of the Earth and—Me

Communist League, which enlightened us on various important political matters. Articles included: *King Government Prepares for War*, by Oscar Ryan; *Fight the Navy League*, by Joe Silver; *Capitalist Sports and the Coming War*, by Cyril Andrews; *Young Pioneer Convention Draws Near*; Editorials by Charles Marriott, (5¢ a copy, 50¢ a year).

I was taking my job as editor of the wall newspaper very seriously. Painstakingly, I drew lines down my sheet and printed carefully (not having a typewritter) the banner headline and the sub-headings on each column of my first editon of the *Young Communist Bugle*. Alas there was to be but one one edition! When I proudly presented my *magnum opus* to the branch meeting, Charlie Marriott, perhaps trying to make an impression, took a pencil and scribbled all over it, the drapery rope by which it was hanging broke, and the whole issue fell to the floor and lay there. Too embarrassed to retrieve it, I watched the members walk around it without caring at the end of the meeting.

"Don't worry," one of the comrades said, "you remain the editor even after it has stopped publication."

The Young Communist League, however, had innumerable goodies for people willing to work and I was quickly elected to a new post: I was to help with the Young Pioneers, who met once a week, on Sundays.

The Young Pioneers, aged 8 to 14, were the movement's answer to the Boy Scouts, Girl Guides and the Sunday Schools. Unfortunately, Pioneer activities were patterned on those of the Young Communist League, which in turn patterned its activities on those of the Communist Party, except that the former had more picnics.

Thus, the Young Pioneers held a meeting once a week, elected a chairman for the meeting and followed a formal agenda, with Minutes, New Business, Reports, Good and Welfare—the works.

The young comrades surprised me. I was 18; most of them were 14 years old and very developed. They certainly knew more about the movement than I did. Some of them were born in it. Lilly Himmelfarb, Rose Kashtan, Simeon Levine, Albert Soren, Eva Blugeman, were very knowledgeable, very gifted young people who snickered a little at their new 'leader.'

However, I was sent down by the League to instruct them and they tolerated me. They showed me, very kindly and gently, what I was to instruct them in and how.

Life a la Jimmy Higgins

(The Young Pioneers whose leader I was to be somewhat later at a summer camp near Sudbury, Ontario, were not as kind when they found out that their camp counsellor sent from Toronto could not swim. They pushed a big log in the lake, my way, and paid no further attention to me. I learned to swim.)

I had little to offer the Pioneers in the Toronto group except to be there. They discussed New Business, which always meant fund raising. Money had to be collected for a Young Pioneer Convention scheduled in the not too distant future. A concert was discussed and organized for December 30, 1928. The advertisement, drawn up myself, appeared in *The Worker*. It bravely announced:

> TORONTO WORKERS! COME TO THE
> PIONEER CONVENTION CONCERT
> SUNDAY, DECEMBER 30TH AT 8:30
> P.M. ALHAMBRA HALL, 450 SPADINA
> AVENUE, RECITATIONS—MUSIC—
> OUT OF TOWN SPEAKERS

Finally the day of the concert arrived and I was the most surprised and pleased person in the world to see the hall actually full. (It held about 450 people.) Three Young Pioneers recited in unison *The Song of the Shirt*. Two recited alternate stanzas of *Looting the Inheritance*:

> *Could one abstract oneself and see*
> *The human race possessing earth*
> *He might find Private Property*
> *A source of tears, a source of mirth.*
>
> *He might behold earth's fertile lands*
> *Held by the living race through use;*
> *In spite of Property's commands*
> *To enforce a system's vast abuse.*
>
> *For, being born, man nothing brings*
> *Takes naught away — His little hour*
> *Is filled with grasping many things,*
> *The yellow Gold, the place of Power.*

The Wretched of the Earth and—Me

The earth is property of ALL
Who at this moment breathe and live
But we into illusion fall,
And to false dreams allowance give,
Permitting certain men to own,
To keep, bequeath the common store
Till laws of Property are known
Enslaving us forever more.

The earth is given us in charge
To use, make better, for a day;
To pass on to our sons—enlarge
Against the beast, the human sway.

But, from a closer view, alas,
We see a small predacious band
Enthroned and called the Master Class
Loot the resources of the Land.

—St. Jean

A 14-year-old violinist trained by Comrade Duffy played *Humoresque* and there were speeches by the out-of-town Pioneer personages, as promised.

The concert opened and closed with the *Internationale*, rendered by six members of the Labor League Mandolin orchestra. A collection was taken up which yielded $65 in quarters, dimes and nickels, of which $25 had to be paid for the rental of the hall.

I was ecstatic.

"The hall was full," I recounted to Oscar Ryan, who, as national secretary of the Young Communist League, was responsible for all the activities of the Young Pioneers, "And there were even some gentlemen in black derby hats who looked very important."

"Oh, they weren't gentlemen, Minnie. One of them was Detective Nursey, head of the 'Red Squad,' and the other was either Detective Mann or Simpson. General Draper, the chief of police, sent them to keep an eye on us. You were lucky they let you take up a collection."

Since the 'Young Pioneers' was a national body, Pioneer organizations in various cities participated in the same events. The concert held in

Life a la Jimmy Higgins

Montreal, however, as reported in *The Worker*, was much more varied and richer in its cultural offerings than the one in Toronto:

> A concert was held on Sunday, December 16, 1928, at the Prince Arthur Hall.
> It opened with the *Internationale* played by the Pioneer Mandolin Orchestra. There were: Recitations by Suzanne Rosenberg; A Dance by Yetta Krause; A Dance by Annie Blanshay and Bessie Fine; A Mass Recitation called *The Clock* , in which Anne Blanshay, Bessie Fine and Annie Teitelman took part, portraying the terrible conditions of the workers.
> There was a piano solo by Dan Braitman, pyramids and a Christmas play. Comrade William Kashtan greeted the Young Pioneers in the name of the Young Communist League.

I continued going to the Young Pioneer meetings every Sunday but I felt there was mighty little leadership that I was providing.

What we supplied the Young Pioneers was unabashed Communist political ideology but our methods left much to be desired. It was not that there was not enough in history and culture of the land to provide inspiration and education for children. It was that at this stage we were not sufficiently skilled or educated to know how to achieve such integration, nor did we have the necessary educational and recreational aids or resources.

General Draper need not have worried too much about the Young Pioneers. Our efforts were very slow, laborious and only partly successful. What we did accomplish, perhaps, was to develop in the children a sense of caring for the good of all (we did limit this to the working class only) of seeking justice for the oppressed, of being self-reliant and irreverent towards constituted authority. It seems to have stood them in good stead in later life.

We relied on the 'language' organizations to influence large numbers of the young by means of involving them in the richness of their own ethnic culture. The Finnish organization (always called the F.O.) had their children's groups based on the teaching of the Finnish language, drama and—always—gymnastics.

The Ukrainian organization concentrated on their Ukrainian literary traditions, on music, dancing and wonderful choir singing. They trained

The Wretched of the Earth and—Me

generations of Ukrainian dancers and singers who, in turn, passed these skills and aptitudes on to their children.

There were others providing youth with the same sort of politically-oriented ethnic cultural background.

Because I had friends there, I knew about the *Peretz Shule*, for instance, run by the Workmen's Circle, whose members went back in their experience and know-how to the organization of these schools in the U.S.A. in 1916. Their aim was to teach Yiddish and spread wide the best traditions of Jewish culture, at the same time being humanitarian, non–religious and socialist (see *World of our Fathers*, Irving Howe).

How I envied them their pedagogical aids, their trained teachers, their special books meant for the children of radical Jewish parents, their skill in spreading far and wide the influence of such giants of Jewish literature as Sholem Aleichem, I.L. Peretz and Mendele Mokher Sforim.

The Jewish left wing was not far behind. It set up the Morris Winchevsky School to teach Yiddish and the secular history of the Jewish people and to open up to the children the rich literary lore of *Yiddishkeit* (Jewish Life), always with a decided bow to the left. Winchevsky, himself, was a brilliant Yiddish poet. He was a friend of William Morris and was active in the early days of the Trade Union Movement.

A children's camp came into being, cheekily named *Naivelt* (New World) in answer to the Peretz Shule's *Youngvelt* (Young World). It soon developed an adult section and was a huge success from the very beginning.

Every Sunday trucks of visitors, and campers, would set out from the Labor League at Brunswick and College and make the short trip to Eldorado Park (near Brampton), leaving the campers and bringing the happy but tired visitors back at the end of the day.

Other camps of the same sort were in existence in the countryside not far from Toronto run by the Ukrainian and Finnish-language organizations where children of members could go for weeks of country life.

Swimming, some arts and crafts, drama, music and story-telling were often part of the program. There were facilities for adult attendance, some members had cottages there and the Finnish organization had set up a sauna and a kitchen with very good coffee.

All these camps had their core of Young Pioneers and we saw to it that they were drawn into 'general activity,' such as reported by *The Worker* on July 20, 1929:

Life a la Jimmy Higgins

WORKERS' CHILDREN'S CONFERENCE
IS PART OF FIGHT AGAINST WAR

A Children's Conference initiated by the Young Pioneers for the sending of a Children's Delegation to the U.S.S.R. took place Friday, July 6th at the Labor League Headquarters. Comrade Albert of the Young Pioneers and Comrade Mike of the Youth Section of the ULFTA (Ukrainian Labor-Farmer Temple Association) were nominated.
Workers! Support the children. We must raise $250 before the 15th of July. The sending of a delegation depends on you!
Donations to date:
Freda..50¢

At the English Branch of the Young Communist League we were busy with inside and outside acitvities. Sometimes we invited everyone to a dance, urging:

COME TO THE GRAND DANCE
SATURDAY APRIL 28
ALHAMBRA HALL
450 SPADINA AVENUE
ADMISSION 35¢

The campaign against the 'ever-looming imperialist war' was not forgotten either. (It ceased looming and became a reality 10 years later.)

MASS PROTEST MEETING
AGAINST MACKENZIE KING'S
DESTROY ERS. FRIDAY, DECEMBER
21 AT ALHAMBRA HALL.
SPEAKER: STEWART SMITH,
JUST RETURNED FROM MOSCOW.
ADMISSION: FREE

Or, in case one had a free Sunday:

COMMUNIST FORUM

The Wretched of the Earth and—Me

>TORONTO, SUNDAY SEPTEMBER 21
>ALHAMBRA HALL:
>THE INDIAN REVOLUTION
>ALL WELCOME!
>
>(*The Worker*, Saturday, September 20, 1928)

Sometimes we fraternized with the Communist Party and attended their 'affairs.' All gatherings of a non-political nature were called 'affairs,' of which there were many varieties. These affairs kept us very busy. They were all advertised in *The Worker*:

>THE ENGLISH SECTION OF THE
>COMMUNIST PARTY WILL HOLD A
>BOX SOCIAL ON FRIDAY, APRIL 27TH
>AT ST. CLAIR AVE. W. CORNER
>GREENLAW.
>THERE WILL BE MUSIC, SINGING,
>DANCING AND REFRESHMENTS.
>A RAFFLE WILL BE HELD OF SOME
>BEAUTIFUL HANDWORK, AND OF A
>LENIN PLAQUE.
>COME! BRING FRIENDS!

Politically, we were in a state of great innocence. We could at this time read and sell books by Leon Trotsky. Bukharin, who was executed as a traitor by Stalin a few years later, was teaching the working class their ABC of Communism in a paperbound edition for 50¢. Other available books included:

American Imperialism by Jay Lovestone (cloth, 15¢)
Whither England by Leon Trotsky (cloth, $2)
Ethics and the Materialist Conception of History, by Kautsky (60¢)
Dictatorship vs. Democracy by Leon Trotsky (hard cover, 50¢)
Ten Days that Shook the World by John Reed (illustrated cover, 85¢).

Immersed as we were in our own activities, we sometimes came up for air and took a quick glance at the outside world.

Things were not so good. Under the editorship of the brilliant Morris Spector, *The Worker* on April 30, 1927, was registering the fearful, black

Life a la Jimmy Higgins

shadows of the approaching Depression:

VANCOUVER COUNCIL PROTESTS AGAINST ROCK PILE

Protests against the proposed established of a rock pile for relief of the unemployed. . .were registered at the Vancouver Trades and Labour Council.
Toronto painters, members of the Painters and Paper Hangers Union in Toronto, are on strike for a maximum rate of 90 cents an hour. The present rate is 75 cents.

(Saturday, June 18, 1927)

As the months went by the crisis intensified quickly. In 1928 the workforce was no longer asking for more, but was fighting wage cuts.

GIRLS IN DOMINION RUBBER COMPANY STRIKE AGAINST BIG WAGE CUT

Montreal, Que. 200 of the girls employed in the Dominion Rubber Company strike against a 25 per cent wage cut last week.
The organizers of the National Catholic Union got the girls together and they were joined in a couple of days by an additional thousand workers from the factory. They all decided to go back to work Friday, at the old rate of pay and await the decision of a Government Arbitration Board. The minimum wage of the girls is $13 a week.

(*The Worker*, April 16, 1928)

Lynchings in the United States were common and did not raise much excitement or indignation:

THREE NEGROES LYNCHED

Liberty, Miss. July 3, 1928 (U.P.) The third lynching in four days has been recorded in Mississipi today after the execution by a mob of 'Shug' McElwee, negro,

The Wretched of the Earth and—Me

accused of attacking a white girl Monday. The alleged attempt to attack the white girl occured about a week ago and it was said that McElwee had been recognized when his mask slipped from his face.
James and Stanley Beardon were lynched, near Brookhaven, Friday after they had been charged with beating two white men to death.

—Toronto Daily Star, July 9, 1928

Emma Goldman in Toronto

"We are going to the next meeting of the Trades and Labour Council," Charlie Marriott told me. "Want to come along?"

He was undoubtedly trying to make amends for defacing my *Wall Newspaper*, so off we went to 167 Church Street, the headquarters of the TLC of Toronto.

Our aim was to have one of our people introduce a resolution deploring the action of the Senate in rejecting, once more, certain amendments to Section 98 of the Criminal Code.

Section 98 was passed in a great hurry during the scare of the General Strike in 1919 and contained measures against militants in the labour movement that would make a person guilty before the law until he could prove himself innocent, measures that we proclaimed as more suitable for Czarist Russia than democratic Canada.

Unfortunately, our resolution did not get put to the Council at that particular time.

However, I was not sad, for following my usual unhappy tendency to fasten on non-essentials, I found the people attending the meeting more interesting than the discussion. Thus I got to meet Marie Tiboldo, who after the meeting was to be seen standing about with a group of men clustered around her. Marie was the delegate from the International Ladies Garment Workers (ILGW)—the fine embroiderers were an affiliated union.

I had heard of her. She was young and slim and beautiful and had the profile of a Neapolitan cameo. To me she was Mary Shelley (Liberal British writer and author of *Frankenstein*) and Krupskaya (Lenin's widow) and Emma Goldman (Anarchist and active fighter for left-wing causes) all rolled into one, standing as she did at the apex of Romantic Communism (a term of my own that I wisely kept to myself). I looked forward to meeting her again at Communist gatherings, perhaps even at meetings of the English Branch of the Young Communist League.

The Wretched of the Earth and—Me

Marie Tibildo, c. 1930

This, however, was not to be, for Marie Tiboldo was not a Romantic Communist; she was not any kind of Communist at all, nor was she particularly romantic. She was a philosophical anarchist, a follower of Bakunin and Peter Kropotkin and, nearer home, one who found anarchist resoundings in the writings of Emerson, Whitman and Thoreau. She was a disciple of Emma Goldman's and never walked the line over to the Communists. She came from an intellectually-oriented family, people who were striving to find a way to ameliorate the lot of the 'exploited classes.' Her father had been influential in gathering around himself a small philosophical group that met every Sunday following the First World War and during the early '20s.

Beside philosophical anarchism they discussed the Single Tax Movement of Henry George (originally a tax on land values to replace all other taxes) as well as articles in *El Martello*, an American anarchist publication to which Marie's mother subscribed.

This little group eventually made liaison with some members of the Workmen's Circle who also found much to be admired in the philosophy of Bakunin and Kropotkin and who had brought their anarchist ideas

Emma Goldman in Toronto

Emma Goldman, c. 1930

with them from Russia—ideas that, however, were not necessarily in line with the straight socialist inclinations of the Workmen's Circle.

It was a small group of free spirits—a print shop manager, a dress manufacturer, the owner of a knitting plant, minor businessmen all— who gathered at their camp at Lake Wilcox in summer and in Toronto during the winter in the Workmen's Circle premises on Beverly Street near the original offices of the Canadian Institute for the Blind.

Restrained, confining themselves to their philosophical discussions, they admired the 'propaganda of the deed' each in his or her own way but not actively and not publicly. They followed Emma Goldman's activities in the United States closely and discussed whether there was sufficient interest in Toronto to warrant inviting Emma to come to Canada for a series of lectures whose topics would include birth control.

Contraception at that time was a controversial subject and distributing birth control information was a criminal offence. Margaret Sanger had been jailed in the United States for issuing a red hot brochure entitled *What Every Woman Should Know*, which was considered pornographic. (Actually, it was William Sanger, her husband, who was sentenced to jail

The Wretched of the Earth and—Me

for one month for circulating one of his wife's pamphlets; he had handed it to an agent of the militant purists, Anthony Comstock).

Eventually, the little anarchist group gathered up enough courage and money and invited Emma Goldman to Toronto.

Marie Tibaldo was appointed to find a hall for the first lecture on birth control. She approached Dr. Gordon Bates, then head of the Health League of Canada, to obtain use of their Hyegia Hall on Elm Street.

"But who will chair the meeting on birth control?" asked the anarchist sponsors. For such an outrageously controversial subject it was difficult to find a chairman. Besides, they might all be arrested.

Marie volunteered but it was thought to be somewhat *risque* and not quite respectable to have a young woman of nineteen preside at such a gathering.

"It should at least be a married woman" was the general opinion.

Fear of being accused of making birth control information available to single girls, a scandalous idea, pervaded their thoughts. Many were approached, but finally, Mrs. Alice Loeb, president of the International League for Peace and Freedom and a fearless liberal and a mother, agreed to be chairlady.

The meeting was a huge success, as was the dinner tendered by the Tiboldo family for Emma and attended by many notables of the city.

Thus encouraged, the little anarchist group popped the question and invited "E.G.," as she was called, to remain in Toronto, renting a flat for her over a restaurant on the west side of Spadina Avenue.

There she lived for many weeks while delivering a series of talks on Dostoyevsky, Ibsen, Gogol and lecturing as well on women's rights and birth control.

All these meetings were held at Hyegia Hall and were very well attended but the nickels and dimes were not quite enough to cover the rental of the hall, much less of Emma's flat.

"How will Emma live?" asked Marie, appalled. "Emma," said the anarchist comrades, "cares little about money. She'll get along." Nonetheless, money was needed for rent and there were worries.

Often, however, fate is kind to the most unlikely recipients of its largess and thus an 'angel,' a patron of birth control, arose in the land—in Kitchener, actually.

He was A.R. Kaufman, a shoe manufacturer who was concerned about his employees being burdened with large families. Having fewer children would enable them to manage better, he thought, and invited Emma to come to Kitchener and lecture on birth control. This led to the famous Parents' Information Bureau being formed in 1929 to serve all of Canada family planning clinics.

As many as 235,000 women benefitted, it was claimed. Four thousand doctors co-operated, including Dr. Eva Bagshaw of Hamilton, who was one of the most active and devoted.

As the Depression had already projected its dreary shadow and there was unemployment and want, bread and butter and tea were served at the clinics, a friendly and humane approach on the part of the sponsors and Mr. Kaufman.

Having cast some good seeds about and trained and inspired a few followers, Emma Goldman left Toronto and returned to continue her stormy life elsewhere.

Practically since the time of her arrival in 1884 Emma Goildman had never ceased in her tireless endeavours to improve the lot of the unfortunate and the exploited in America.

She had fought alongside the Industrial Workers of the World (IWW) to encourage and defend the newly-formed trades unions. She was involved in the early cloakmakers' strike in New York, and she defended the Haymarket Victims in 1886—when at an anarchist rally in Haymarket Square, Chicago, police and spectators died when a bomb exploded. Six immigrant labour activists were charged with the crime and executed. Emma was a lifelong friend of Alexander Berkman, the unsuccessful assassin of Henry Clay Frick, Chairman of the Carnegie Steel Company, who had locked the workers out during a bitter strike and then had evicted them from company housing. (Berkman served 22 years for his crime.) Emma had fought every battle, organized hundreds of meetings in every city in the U.S., led parades, was writer and publisher of *Mother Earth*, follower of and lecturer in drama, theatre, dance and world literature, adding birth control and the rights of women and homosexuals to her discourses. She functioned as nurse and midwife, earned a living as a corset operator, sewed prison labels in Missouri State Penitentiary, daring to discuss openly methods of contraception, speaking on the failure of Cristianity, with particular emphasis on the personality of the revivalist preacher Billy Sunday. She did not hesitate to hold meetings in defense of the assassin of President McKinley, Leon Cziolgosz. Emma set up Free Speech organizations and No Conscription leagues in 1917. She was fiercely pursued, harrassed, persecuted, and

The Wretched of the Earth and—Me

raided and she had her meetings broken up innumerable times in as many cities. She spent a year in Blackwell's Island Penitentiary, where she was visited in jail at Passover by her grandmother with matzos and gefilte fish.

Sometime friend and follower of Peter Kropotkin and vehement defender of Mooney and Billings—held responsible for a bomb attack during a Preparedness Day parade and sentenced to death and to life imprisonment respectively—Emma Goldman, of course, felt free to form intimate relationships without the encumbrace of marriage and thereby encumbered radicals with the Free Love image for decades! She did meet and collaborate with every militant spirit in the land from Roger Baldwin to Eugene Debs and Morris Hillquit.

Opposing the draft in 1917 she spent her fiftieth birthday and 20 months in Missouri State Prison. Released in 1919 she was ordered deported when her husband's citizenship was revoked. She was put to sea in a leaky boat with Alexander Berkman and 200 other victims of red paranoia. Received in Russia with open arms by the revolutionaries, Emma was swiftly disappointed to see the revolution devouring its children, ends not justifying means, acts of useless violence! Not able to co-operate with Lenin nor Trotsky she made her way to England and thence to Canada,.

It was in the Spanish Civil War that she came into her own where she saw factory and farm collectives, libertarian schools, people's militias and announced joyfully to the Federacion Anarquista Iberica (FAI) "Your revolution will destroy forever the notion that anarchism stands for chaos. She established a support committee in England which included George Orwell, W.H. Auden, Cowper Powys and Rebecca West. In 1938 the Spanish revolution disappointed her once more. She went to Canada again to raise money for the refugees and spent her seventieth birtday in Montreal. On her return to Toronto she suffered a stroke and died on May 18, 1940. US Immigration officials allowed her body entry into the U.S.A. to be buried near the graves of her Haymarket comrades in Chicago's Waldheim cemetery

Marie Tiboldo, on the other hand, went on to serve the cause of the people in a new field, that of the fine embroidery workers of Toronto.

Women's fashions in the '20s called for a great deal of embroidery. No stylishly attired woman would appear in public in a bare frock. It had to be embellished with embroidery, with beads (bugle beads were most desirable), with braid (a countless variety of braid existed), with a mixture of braid and buttons or vari-colored soutache. Blouses, skirts, suits and even coats were thus adorned either by hand or by machine.

Marie had followed this trade since she was sixteen, was skilled at both hand and machine embroidery and had no difficulty obtaining work in the field.

In the shop where she was employed, she was much admired by both employers and workers, as much for her militancy and education as for her physical beauty. Management, however, lost its enthusiasm when Marie called a strike soon after she was hired.

The employers considered the demands for increased wages outrageous, the girls started picketing and soon found themselves locked out.

While Marie led the young women on the picket line in sub-zero temperatures, girl scabs were brought in from across the border.

Marie, however, had friends everywhere.

A telephone call brought photographers, reporters and accusations of "Laxity By Immigration Officials" in the papers. An inquiry into this type of border crossing brought about the deportation of the scabs.

The embroiderers won their strike, coming under the wing of the powerful ILGW. This action won Marie a seat on the District Trades and Labour Council as a delegate from the Embroiderers Union and it was the Trades and Labour Council that sent her to the U.S. to attend A.J. Muste's School for Girls in Industry.

However, fashion being fickle, embroidered garments came and went, leaving Marie without a trade—but not for long.

During World War II, she was employed in the radio tube industry—there, too, organizing a union for the girls who were working for 30 cents an hour. Oddly enough, here she was able to convince her supervisor that an organized shop would benefit everyone and Marie got her union and an improvement in wages without too much striving.

Throughout the years I encountered Marie at various political events. Once, picketing the American Consulate on University Avenue during one of the numerous disagreements we had with the U.S. over its foreign policy ("Get Out of Vietnam" this time), I found myself side by side with Marie. Less afraid now of ideological infection, I boldly questioned her about her politics.

"First of all, I want you to know that the Party does not have a

The Wretched of the Earth and—Me

monopoly on the struggle to make this a better world, so I participate in all activities and campaigns that are good and just, no matter who initiates them," she told me.

That was Marie, a bold categorical statement of her position.

"But what will take place after the revolution?" I asked her anxiously, still expecting this happy event to pop up anytime and present me with problems.

"My departure from the line followed by the Communists concerns the Marxist view of the state," she said. "Karl Marx says that the state, being a tool to maintain power of one class over the other, will wither away when there are no more classes. This is not true. Bakunin was correct in stating that the state becomes more firmly entrenched. Today the Soviet state is stronger; it is not fading or withering away."

I stared at her curiously.

Her hair was graying but she was still beautiful, still slim, still unafraid and obviously still deeply committed.

Always besieged by a string of suitors, she never married.

In the office of a dress manufacturer where I was employed years later, I heard the plaint of one such rejected and frustrated suitor. Knowing of my participation in the labour movement, he inquired if I knew Marie.

"You know, I sell braid to the trade and came across Marie in one of the shops," he related. "I had a tough time getting a date, but I persisted and finally she invited me to her home for a Sunday evening. It wasn't what I wanted but still ... So carrying a bottle of wine and flowers I made my way to her house, where I was let in by her mother. It wasn't the only one. The living room was full of people, mostly men. A hot political conversation was taking place, washed down by Mrs. Tiboldo's homemade Italian wine—you know, sour, dry, just like the discussion. I stayed for a while and then made my way out as soon as I politely could.

"I didn't date her again. Such a pretty girl—to be so political." And he shook his head in regret and disbelief.

I get to go to University

That there was discipline in the Young Communist League in 1927, we found out when we three newly-joined members proposed to pick ourselves up and leave for New York on a lengthy visit, according to plans we had made before dedicating our lives to a sacred cause. (We had just reached our goal of saving up $300 each for the trip.)

"You comrades will have to apply for leave of absences," Sam Carr of the 'District Committee' cooly informed us, "And you may not get permission to go."

Leave of absence? What was that? The dictionary said it was "permission to leave a post of duty."

Sure enough, at the next meeting of the English Branch of the YCL there was a heated discussion on the agenda entitled "leave of absence for comrades Shirley Etlin, Anne Kohen and Minnie Davis" and the resolution that leave be granted barely squeezed through. There were even some charges of favoritism after the meeting.

So impressed were we with the business of discipline that it never occurred to us that we might leave whether we obtained permission or not.

Obviously, we were definitely committed to the Young Communist League, its philosophy and its discipline and were really happy with that sort of allegiance. It made us feel important. It made the time and effort we had put into the work of the movement seem worthwhile and we envisioned momentous tasks awaiting us on our return. We liked it that way and we were pleased that we were on leave of absence.

"Life is real life is earnest, Simple joys are not its goal," I quoted to myself in the train as it chugged away to New York.

"Simmer down, Minnie," cautioned Shirley, herself always cool and detached. But I was boiling with the excitement of life and with what might await us at our destination.

Fortunately, the Depression had not yet extended its paralyzing tentacles throughout the industrial life of New York and we were able to obtain employment as soon as we arrived.

The Wretched of the Earth and—Me

Flatbush Avenue, Brooklyn, N.Y., c. 1927

In Flatbush we found a pleasant three-storied, clapboard house, painted white, where we rented a furnished room each from a very friendly landlady. There were even roses blooming in the garden—very Toronto-like.

No sooner were we settled in than we heard from American friends of A Summer School For Girls In Industry to take place at Barnard College and at Bryn Mawr. We made our applications and, to our surprise, were promptly notified of our acceptance. The classes were to take place almost immediately at Barnard, the women's college of Columbia University, and we promptly quit our jobs.

The Muste group was well fixed financially, and because we were from out of town, the scholarship awarded us was very generous; free tuition, $25 a month each and two meals a day in the school cafeteria. For me, paradise on earth unfolded every day on the campus of Barnard College. The very terms: campus, faculty, college and syllabus were mysterious formulas to open up a magic world.

The summer school was controlled by the faculty and students during the term. It was to co-operate, however, with labour colleges, workers' schools and trade unions in recruiting students and in helping them through the curriculum to achieve an understanding of the industrial problems in their trade. These schools operated at Bryn Mawr, Barnard College and the University of Wisconsin.

First there were the lectures. Ancient and modern history, economics —during which I didn't hesitate to parade my newly-acquired snatches of Marxism—and literature, for which I pompously and presumptuously created a critique of Voltaire under the unusual title of *The Pen is Mightier than the Sword*.

I swallowed it all in huge gulps and became the most unpopular student in class, voraciously studying everything, reading, writing, living in the library, quivering with anxiety to answer all the teachers' questions and taking it all very seriously. (Where was Shirley to suggest "Simmer down, Minnie?" All she said now was, "You're not studying for a BA, you know.")

Not so, the other girls in industry. For them, this two-month stretch was a holiday away from work and very quickly a chasm developed between them and us. They resented these Communist girls from Canada who had received a better scholarship than they did and who, in addition, were obviously favoured by various professors.

"And they're not even working-class, damn it. They're stenographers," was heard in the corridors.

And then there was the faculty. Being education crazy, I was prepared to deify any professor but this was a group of remarkably dedicated, truly high-minded academics who were socialistically inclined and were giving their time freely for what they considered a good cause. I loved them all.

My favorite was Lucille Cohen, at one time a private tutor to the Guggenheim family, a delicately featured, grey-haired tall lady with a soft voice and a kind, gentle approach. She lectured on ancient and modern history.

Balancing her way dexterously between Marxism and the accepted economics of the establishment was Professor Hutchinson, on the staff of Barnard College and remarkably tolerant of my pitiful and impudent attempt to hold forth on "Value, Price and Profit" to the class. Finally, a real author who had just published *Horse Shoe Bottoms*, Tom Tippett, taught creative writing. Miss Charlotte Wilder, sister of Thornton Wilder, author of *The Bridge Of St. Louis Rey*, was on the staff to instruct us in drama.

For some mysterious reason, the faculty had singled out the three

The Wretched of the Earth and—Me

Canadian girls for their attention. We were invited to dine at Miss Cohen's elegant apartment, where we met her father, an aristocratic Hebrew scholar whose family had been part of the Sephardic community (the Spanish section of European jewry) in New York for generations. Professor Hutchinson took us out to lunch, and then the librarian, Miss Betty Martin, suggested a Sunday visit to her apartment.

Betty Martin was the type of southern 'gal' I had only envisioned in fiction—tall, hefty, blonde, not too committed to politics yet liberal, full of fun and very tolerant in her approach to everyone and everything. When we were made loud and giddy by unaccustomed pre-lunch cocktails in the July heat, she simply pushed us under the shower, where the cold water sobered us up quickly enough. Then she served us a very elegant lunch.

It was she who explained the reason for our popularity with the staff. "You see," she drawled, "you gals sort of headed the lists in the intelligence tests." (These were intended to establish ability to absorb the courses).

We absorbed and eagerly savoured the academic environment around us. The school atmosphere was there, to some extent, even though the buildings were unoccupied and the lecture rooms vacant. We were given swimming instructions. I saw a pool for the first time and learned how to dive, forgotten since.

We presented a play, dramatized by ourselves from a long poem by Edna St. Vincent Millay, whose poetry was on everyone's lips at that time. I had been given a slim volume entitled *Figs from Thistles* by Charlie Marriott before I left Toronto and I knew many of her poems by heart.

> *My candle burns at both ends*
> *It will not last the night*
> *But oh, my friends and ah, my foes*
> *It gives a lovely light.*

It wasn't me but I could admire such a devil-may-care outlook on life, in principle.

We explored New York City.

One Saturday night Shirley said: "Let's go to Harlem."

We were not far from Harlem, our new apartment building being located somewhere around 177th Street and Broadway. We felt that this was the time and place to enter another phase of the movement, to go where the black comrades were.

I get to go to University

Harlem, N.Y., c. 1927

There were no black students among the girls in industry sent by the American labour movement to the college and we had not met any comrades who were black, called at that time 'colored.'

Where were the black members of the Young Communist League in New York? We tried making contacts with some YCLers.

Unfortunately, the Communist movement in New York did not approve of us. A.J. Muste and his school were frowned upon as being reformist; monsters of heresy were believed to lurk in the halls of learning that he directed and we were cooly received, indeed snubbed. We even received a letter of disapproval from the Young Communist League in Toronto. Consequently, we stayed away from Communist circles.

Our fellow students, on the other hand, boycotted us, among other reasons, for being too left.

Therefore, we went to Harlem on our own.

We wandered the streets on Saturday nights, revelling in the sounds, the colour, the geniality, the warmth and in the friendliness of everyone. We went to the movies, which included a vaudeville show consisting of a chorus line of lovely black girls, and had our Saturday night splurge—

The Wretched of the Earth and—Me

dinner in a local café. Then we walked back to our apartment or took the subway for a few stops.

There were other experiences to be had.

Every city has its shrines and when we had time, we visited the Communist tourist attractions.

We found mass meetings of all sorts being held in Union Square and ran to Cooper Union to gaze in awe at the walls, which had absorbed the passionate speeches of so many early leaders of labor. Cooper Union—only 18 years earlier an amazing private college founded by Peter Cooper for the improvement of the working classes. Later becoming the Peoples' Institute, drawing thousands every year to its concerts and its lectures on Socialism, on Darwin, on anything that might stretch the mind. Maxim Gorki lectured in the Cooper Union and so did Emma Goldman.

We recounted to each other how the International Ladies Garment Workers Union on November 22, 1909, called a meeting of the shirtwaist makers—who were, at that time, 99 per cent girls—at Cooper Union. Although Local 25 had slightly more than 100 members, thousands came to the meeting, spilling out into other halls.

Girls from the Triangle Waist Company were there, a shop that locked its employees in at work. In 1911, a disastrous fire occurred in the plant, destroying the whole building and burning to death 146 young workers, mostly Jewish and Italian girls.

At the memorable Cooper Union meeting, venerable leaders of the trade union movement, led by Samuel Gompers, addressed the crowd, sometimes urging caution. Suddenly a frail teenage girl, Clara Lemlich, who had been picketing day after day at a strike-bound plant, pushed to the front and burst into Yiddish:

"I am one of those girls striking against intolerable conditions....What we are here for is to decide whether to strike or not. I offer a resolution: That a general strike be called — NOW."

A contagion of excitement swept the meeting, people screaming and stamping, and when the chairman asked for a seconder, the whole crowd shouted its approval. The chairman, Benjamin Feigenbaum, shaken by the outburst, cried out: "Do you mean it in good faith? Will you take the old Jewish oath?"

Thousands of hands went up.

"If I turn traitor to the cause I now pledge, may this hand wither from the arm I raise." (See: *World of Our Fathers*, Irving Howe.)

I get to go to university

That was in the Cooper Union.

There were wonders of the present day, too. In the Bronx we visited a co-operative housing project funded by that mother and father of labour unions, the ILGW; the free, outdoor concerts at Lewishon Stadium, though not exactly Communist in content, brought out all the working people on a Sunday afternoon in fine weather.

Truly we led an enchanted life in New York during the summer of 1927 —we didn't know how truly privileged we were.

Columbia University had feet of clay. It did not open its doors wide to all who craved knowledge but, as did other universities, set up quotas. Between 1920 and 1922, "Columbia University instituted regional quotas and, since most Jewish applicants came from the East, this cut the proportion of Jewish students from 40 per cent to 22 per cent," Irving Howe wrote in *World of Our Fathers.*

"It was commonly charged against Jewish students that they studied so assiduously 'they memorized their books.' Jews made non-Jewish students uncomfortable and thereby threatened the social poise of college life."

Ludwig Lewisohn, a man of literary distinction who had finished his graduate work at Columbia in 1922, encountered repeated rejections from heads of English departments throughout the country, some of whom did not even bother to veil their true reasons. From his own professor at Columbia, Lewisohn received a chilly note remarking on "how terribly hard it is for a man of Jewish birth to get a good position," Howe relates.

Only two of us returned to Toronto after our three-month leave of absence. Shirley remained in New York but as she engaged actively in YCL work she was forgiven her transgression.

Another Canadian attending the School for Girls in Industry, although at the Bryn Mawr location, was Marie Tiboldo of Toronto.

Signs and Portents

Taking time off from my tasks as bookkeeper for the Vanity Fair Dress Company, I set out on a beautiful morning in July 1928 as delegate to the Fifth National Convention of the Young Communist League being held at the Don Hall on Broadview Avenue in Toronto. I was wearing a black, artificial silk dress on which I had sewn a dainty green organdy collar, being still addicted to feminine fashions and frilly touches.

My high-heeled shoes clicked their enthusiasm as I hurried under the vivid green of the trees lining Palmerston Avenue and the little houses wearing their tiny aprons of jade lawn seemed to smile their approval.

"A beautiful day and the right activity for it," I happily announced to myself. "But could I have been just as happy if I had been going to a convention of the Young Judeans? Suppose I had stuck with Nellie Orloff—a charismatic and much-loved youth leader who briefly won our attention and attendance at a few meetings, just before Diana Shiner invited us to that little reading circle—or suppose I was going to a Bible conference?"

No, definitely not that. And I rushed for the streetcar stop at the corner of College Street.

There were 48 delegates to the YCL Convention from all parts of Canada, according to the report I sent in to *The Worker* (Saturday, July 13, 1928).

From the West, most of them came riding the rods—the practice of obtaining a handhold or a foothold on the rods underneath a railroad car, which, unfortunately, sometimes led to the loss of a limb. However, the greatest sensation was created by Mabel Marlowe (her self-chosen pseudonym), who, dressed in blue denim jeans, which no one else wore yet, hitched a ride in a boxcar with the rest of the delegation from Port Arthur (now Thunder Bay, Ontario).

I stared at Mabel in dismay and felt very *bourgeoise* (and dowdy) in my black rayon 'silk' with its frilly organdy collar.

It was only later that the correct wear for the rebel girl established itself to be a leather jacket and very flat heels. Being very short-legged and sort of square, even when very skinny, I resisted the style for a long time, but in vain. Leather jackets and flat heels were very much more useful on the picket line and at police confrontations and they became *de rigueur* wear for a long time.

The strong Montreal delegation included two French-Canadians at whom we gazed with awe and whose presence we interpreted as an "indication of the radicalization of this most exploited section of the young workers of Canada."

We had delegates from the mines of Cape Breton, N.S. (Murdoch Clarke) and from Winnipeg. Included were many girls, a sign of the politicization of women. (We were great believers in signs and portents and were constantly on the lookout for such phenomena.)

The convention actually represented a good cross-section of Canadian *pot pourri*—of Anglo Saxon (much made of), Ukrainian, Finnish, Jewish, everything but native Indian. We had not been told about that minority and no one was sufficiently original or courageous to think of that most dispossessed and oppressed section of Canadian society.

The secretary, Oscar Ryan, opened the convention, a presidium was elected in the best parliamentary manner and the delegates set down to the task of mapping out its policies in relation to the problems of the youth of Canada. Of course, the agenda and the main policies had previously been laid down at the National Executive Committee with the help and approval of the Communist Party.

We were not encouraged to oppose, criticize or improve on the 'line' laid down but to discuss it and accept it. The main theme of the convention was the fight against the coming Imperialist war—we were a bit early, 10 years in fact—defend the Soviet Union and prepare for class war against the bourgeoisie.

We carried on talking along these lines and dug deeply into world social analysis.

After all, did not the very structure of capitalism lead to wars? Were we not still in the period of the imperialist division of the world into colonies and spheres of influence? Was it not a fact that the existence of a socialist-structured society—the Soviet Union—posed a threat to the capitalist world and therefore the latter must be trying to destroy this rival system that offers its workers a solution to all their problems?

The workers of the world must strive to retain the existence of socialism in the Soviet Union, a system that has so frightened the

The Wretched of the Earth and—Me

capitalists that they have by now agreed to many social benefits and can be made to disgorge more of their ill-gotten gains if pushed by radical fighting unions.

On these premises we could accept anything.

However, I was worried about the dearth of proposals that would bring immediate benefit to the working-class youth, or even be understood as affecting them.

"If I had to explain to a young person in a shop about this convention," I said to Charlie Marriott at the end of the sessions, "And he said to me, 'What's in it for me?' I'd have to say 'Nothing, immediately!' So what's the good of it?"

"That is all too simplistic," said Charlie. "It's unpoliticized talk. It's bourgeois garbage. The Russian revolution would never had taken place if one talked like that!"

Charlie had a way with words and that was the end of the argument.

The convention dragged on and on for three days. We talked endlessly about the coming struggles, winning over large sections of the working youth for a revolutionary role in the coming war, etc.

Everyone talked of these things in turn (supported the line). It was a relief when one delegate strayed a bit and all the other speakers could attack him, pointing out that deviations are floating on miasmic currents in the convention and we must stamp them out immediately.

The convention fever, not very high at any time, rose somewhat at this and then the National Executive Committee (henceforth known as the NEC) was chosen. We all wanted the honor of being elected and we tried to select those who could best carry out the line laid down by the convention. Needless to say, the young delegate who had livened up the convention by straying from the line was not nominated.

The report in *The Worker* stated that the NEC consisted of new proletarian elements, such as (Fred Rose) Rosenberg, Murdock Clarke, Waxman (Paul Phillips), Mary Gilbert and Dora Leibovich. Fred who was a future communist MP from Montreal, was eventually charged with passing secret material to the Soviet Union, tried, convicted, and deported to Poland, where he eventually died.

They deserved a better guide than the line we laid down.

However, this was July 1928.

We had not read the portents right for the economic Depression, we did not emphasize that it was practically upon us. However, every one

Signs and Portents

The author, c. 1928

of the delegates returning home became a leader in the struggle against hunger and joblessness and against the indifference of the powers that be to the hunger that stalked the land.

The convention lasted until the wee hours of the morning. Some delegates found the costume room of the Finnish Organization's Theatre Section and, without asking permission, wrapped themselves in the most voluminous outfits they could find and stretched out on the floor.

No one offered me a costume or helped me to reach one and after waiting in vain for some attention I pulled down a Pierrette costume, its skimpiness helping me not a bit to dispel the pre-dawn chill.

"It serves you right," I told myself, remembering the insouciance with which I had set out in the morning. "You should at least have brought a sweater."

I was not only angry, I was depressed as well, being unsure as to whether this was the right place for me or the right thing to do. I was worried about the future, which looked nebulous—dark and mostly frightening.

Rebel Girl

The rebel girl, the rebel girl
To the working class
She's a perfect pearl

— Joe Hill

I was envious of the comrades and of those families who were totally dedicated to the movement. It denoted a way of life that had its acceptable and unacceptable behaviour clearly indicated, definitely outlined.

Wearing fashionable or expensive clothing was out; rummage sale clothes were in. Living north of Davenport Road was *bourgeois*; College Street and its environs was approved of, while the east end (not too far east) or the west end around Brock, Pacific or near Delaney Crescent, where Tim Buck, the General Secretary of the Communist Party, lived, was definitely desirable.

Travelling, going to concerts, drinking alcohol, dining in restaurants (except for 'coffee and' at the Rose Café on College and Spadina or at the Homestead Restaurant on Spadina near College) was acceptable in minute quantities. For who, except the *bourgeoisie*, could afford much of that?

I kept to these unwritten rules but transgressed when it came to friends.

"Why do you want to hang around with those *bourgeois* types?" my good friend Sonia would say to me. For I had friends outside and stubbornly clung to them for years. This was frowned upon as creating a funnel through which bourgeois, even anti-Communist, ideas might seep in.

"They might become sympathizers," I told Sonia.

"Yea? When?"

"I'm working on it."

I was always working on it and that is why I was not even half way on the road to total commitment—like Lilly Himmelfarb, for instance.

It was axiomatic in the Young Communist League that Lilly

Rebel Girl

Himmelfarb was devoted to the movement to the exclusion of everything else. The movement was everything; she did not envisage any other way of life. But it was easy for Lilly. She owed her total commitment to her mother, who had introduced the political solution and Communist ideals to a family condemned to poverty and hard work.

Mrs. Himmelfarb toiled in a factory all her life, trudging to her Spadina Avenue job summer and winter, a dull, hard existence eased only by her activities in the movement. This after-work political life spelled an escape from the workaday world, providing something to think about, to look forward to, a change of pace. She believed that the rat race she was in would not be the lot of countless mothers if she, and others like her, just worked hard enough for the future.

To this cause she devoted herself and offered up her son—her first-born, Victor—and her daughter, Lillian, but not her husband. Somehow he rebelled against this devotion of the whole family to an ideal in which he was not quite sure he could believe.

"Maybe!" was all he would say in answer to her arguments. He was hard-of-hearing and a great deal of what went on—the discussions, the table talk, the decisions, the meetings, the visitors coming and going—were a closed world to him and he turned his back on it all.

Lillian, however, imbibed Communist ideology with her Pablum.

In no time at all she was in the Young Pioneers and it was during this period that the organization in Toronto was at its finest. She had a good speaking voice, a voice that had ample volume and could transmit every nuance of emotion she felt. Some said that when you listened to Lillian you could hear the misery and sorrow of the underprivileged, of all those who lived at the bottom of the social ladder.

Lillian was arrested 14 times, jailed only once. That was in 1929, when she was 16 going on 17 years old.

At that time Canada was selling scrap iron to Japan, considered a fiercely competitive and expansionist power. The Communists contended that the scrap iron was being fashioned into shells, weapons to be used, perhaps, against us. We anticipated war with imperialist Japan and were opposed to supplying it with the wherewithal to kill "the flower of our working-class youth."

It was for this reason that we wore only lisle stockings, the silk ones from Japan being on a self-imposed boycott list.

Came August 4, 1929 our proclaimed Day Against War and Fascism,

The Wretched of the Earth and—Me

the anniversary when World War One was ignited.

In Southern Ontario the Party planned a "Hands Across the Border" action to show international solidarity and to properly mark the day. Everyone would have a chance to participate.

The YCL never discriminated against us girls, as females. We could always get the most difficult, outrageously dangerous assignment without the least opposition to us on the ground that we were merely women.

The "Hands Across the Border" was therefore organized without any discrimination. Even I was not blackballed on account of my squeaky, thin voice, which could not be heard except by five people standing very close. We received our not-too-detailed instructions—with which we were in full agreement, of course.

"You, Minnie, go to St. Catharines and hold a noon-hour shop-gate meeting at McKinnon Industries."

"You, Lillian, go across the bridge, meet the American comrades half way, walk back with them and hold a meeting on the other side."

Paul Philips was to go and stir up the workers on this issue in other municipalities on the Niagara Peninsula.

Presumably, we were all to gather together on the American side, each one of us bringing workers who were aroused on this issue with us like so many Pied Pipers. As a plan on paper it might have been brilliant but as logistics it was rotten. It just couldn't work.

On the morning of August 4, led by Oscar Ryan, who had managed to hire a truck (we always travelled by truck, unless we were not quite so lucky and had to hitch-hike), about 20 of us set out to explain things to the workers and to carry them with us psychologically and perhaps even physically to the meeting in Niagara Falls, N.Y., there to make international history.

I was dropped off at McKinnon Industries in time for the noon break. I had only one comrade with me, I didn't even have a chair to stand on (there were never any soapboxes around for us soapbox orators: What were soapboxes anyway? I never saw one) and my spirits were at the bottom of my feet. How does one gather a crowd around oneself, for Heaven's sake?

But I didn't have to worry! Someone found an orange crate, I stood on it and after a few words out of my mouth, people came closer so they could hear and still others gathered around to see the crazy girl standing up there and more came to find out why the crowd was gathering.

My voice was thin and in an attempt to project it I shouted. I was not a success as a speaker but a girl standing up 'orating' was an attraction and they listened politely while I explained about the scrap iron and the danger of war and fascism and about the lisle stockings. I even got a few "hear, hears" when the police, in the shape of a paddy wagon and two cars full of St. Catharines' finest, rushed up. Apparently, management feared that the 'reds' were really invading and telephoned for help.

After casting an expert eye over the invasion, the police thought it safe to send the paddy wagon back but adequate forces in two cars waited for me, whilst I, with an eye on the clock and the other on the defenders of the state drew the conclusions for the crowd—huge by this time—how the bosses were lining up with the imperialists, else what are the cops doing here instead of chasing bootleggers?

The one o'clock whistle blew, the employees filed back into the shop well-satisfied with the diversion and I was invited into one of the cars for a little ride to the police station.

They told me to sit on a bench in the station and wait. I waited for two hours and was finally ushered into a presence.

The Chief of Police himself sat behind a desk, fat and important, stern and mad.

"This is St. Catharines, known as the Garden City, the City of Flowers. This is a very clean town and we don't want your kind here. GET OUT FAST AND NEVER COME BACK AGAIN. NOW GET OUT!"

They escorted me back to the police car, drove to the highway and unceremoniously dumped me on the side of the road, miles from anywhere.

It took some time to orient myself and to find my way to the appointed reconnoitering in Niagara Falls, Ontario, for I had to hitch hike all the way, fearful of the police.

In the meantime, Lillian Himmelfarb had reached the first bridge and tried to enter the United States.

Having a stool pigeon called Goussep with her didn't seem to make much difference and she was turned back. She made it across the second bridge, however, and astoundingly found the American comrades with whom she was supposed to rendezvous.

A meeting commenced on the parkside nearest the bridge and Lillian was introduced as the first speaker of this international gathering. She

The Wretched of the Earth and—Me

didn't get very far. The police, not as polite as the St. Catharines lot, didn't stand around and wait for her to finish but made their 'pinch' right there and then and she was quickly driven off to Buffalo, N.Y., and lodged in jail overnight.

In the morning, a judge in Lockport, N.Y., didn't hesitate one second to sentence Lillian Himmelfarb, 16 years old going on 17, to 30 days in jail for 'illegal entry.' She had had no defence counsel and could not get the ridiculous bail of $30,000 that would have provided the American comrades with enough time to find a defence lawyer.

She commenced to serve her sentence alone in a cell, from which she was released the next day to wander an empty corridor. For the first few days there were no other female prisoners and she had the freedom of the place. She was frightened and then bored, ate the meals they brought to her cell, read newspapers, walked up and down.

Then they raided a call house and she was more than frightened, she was terrified, for the corridor filled with prostitutes, young and old, rough and voluble. They gathered around her, questioning:

"What ya in fer?"

"Thirty days," said Lillian.

"No, stupid, what did ya do?"

"Oh," said Lillian, "I spoke at a meeting."

"What did ya get fer it?"

"Thirty days."

"No, stupid, how much did they pay ya for speakin'?"

"Nothing, you don't get paid...."

"Listen to this girls, she did it for nothin'. Listen kid, never do it for nothin.'"

She was their source of amusement during the rest of her stay, every minute and every hour of which she had to serve as she did not get released one day before the expiration of her sentence.

At the end of the 30 days she was freed and conducted in a car to the Canadian border. The young officer escorting her, apparently under the impression that she was in the same profession as the other inmates, made offers.

"After all," he reasoned, "you've been without it for 30 days."

"You leave me alone or I'll scream," said Lillian. Communist or not, a scream was a girl's best weapon and it was effective.

"It was only an offer" was the mild rejoinder and he escorted her into

Rebel Girl

the office of the Canadian immigration officials, where her mother was waiting with her birth certificate.

The rest of us did manage on that August 4th to meet together with Oscar Ryan in Niagara Falls, Ontario.

And we left that city at the end of the day well enough but ingloriously.

Our truck with its strident banners of RALLY TO THE 'HANDS ACROSS THE BORDER MEETING' ON THIS INTERNATIONAL DAY AGAINST WAR AND FASCISM had attracted an unwelcome WASP in the person of Red Hill, the hero of the Niagara Gorge.

Self-appointed defender of the clean way of life for the peninsula, he gathered some youths as brave and clean as he and as we started on our way home, they chased after us in trucks and cars, pelting us with stones and littering the highway with broken bottles, overripe fruit and rotten tomatoes for miles beyond the escarpment area.

We arrived in Toronto more or less safely, leaving one brave soldier of the cause behind in jail.

Lillian Himmelfarb was first arrested while picketing in front of the American Consulate on University Avenue. She was only fifteen then and had just "graduated" from the Young Pioneers into the Young Communist League. The year was 1928 at the time of the agony of Sacco and Venzetti, anarchists sentenced to death and executed in the United States and regarded as innocent by many, and the signs carried asked for a fair trial for the two.

The stool pigeon picketing with her this time was no other than the famed Sergeant Leopold of the RCMP, known in the Party as comrade Esselwein. All the picketers were arrested—Lillian, Annie Buller, Oscar Ryan and Esselwein. Taken to the Lombard Street police station, perhaps because the catch included one very big fish called Esselwein, the whole lot was released.

The second time she was arrested was with Dora Leighton and Becky Lapidus for distributing throw-aways in front of a firm accused of exploiting young girls, Barrymore Cloth. The leaflets asked the girls to fight against low wages and exploitation and because the word "fight" was included, all arrested were charged with sedition. A clever lawyer won acquittal for the lot when he was able to convince the judge that the word "fight" was not necessarily seditious. The movement hailed the judge's ruling as an important step forward in the annals of justice.

Lilly was arrested again in the company of J.B. Salsberg, a popular

The Wretched of the Earth and—Me

leader in the needle trades, union activist and MPP in the Ontario Legislature in the 'thirties, at an open-air meeting on Pacific and Dundas Sts. in 1929. The charge was 'unlawful assembly,' much to the disgust of "J.B.," who argued that, in his opinion, there would have to be at least 20 people before a gathering could be called an assembly. There weren't 20 people there.

The police dropped the charges but upbraided the future MP for misleading Lillian Himmelfarb by allowing such a young girl to "make a show of herself."

Lillian was singled out by the Y.C.L. to be sent to organize the cannery workers in that "garden city" of St. Catharines, at that time the most exploited and low-paid group of workers, consisting mainly of women and girls.

There, she found herself a room at a comrade's house for $4 a week, breakfast included, but as no one sent her any money (there was no union or other organization to back her) that was often the only meal of the day she got.

Occasionally a local comrade would invite her for supper but not many could afford to do that.

She did get a free meal when she was thrown into the Welland County Jail—having been arrested for speaking in a public park about matters "strictly local," that is the exploitation of local cannery workers.

She was released but the town's newspaper hurt Lillian's feelings acutely by talking about the "young agitator with a pimply face" and even the acknowledgement that out of the mouth of babes one can sometimes hear the truth, didn't heal the insult.

The mayor, a Mr. Daley, was furious at this unfavorable publicity for his "city of flowers." Meeting Lillian on the street one day — he had previously made her acquaintance—he stopped, turned around and castigated her as being a "red menace."

Lillian had had enough of insults.

"I'M NOT A MENACE," she yelled back. 'I'M, I'M, well I'm just red." Lillian loved the movement, as did her mother. It provided both with their happiest moments, perhaps none on a higher level than the Monday morning when we held a meeting of the National Executive Committee of the Young Communist League in her living room, this being the time when the Communist Party and the Y.C.L. were outlawed. Mrs. Himmelfarb, proud of this important gathering under her roof, rushed into the kitchen to prepare some lunch.

Rebel Girl

There wasn't much there. She found a bag of potatoes, however, and set to peeling and grating and then frying dozens of pancakes in her little kitchen while we planned for the revolutionary movement in her living room. Of such stuff were the big moments made.

Except for one thing. Mother and daughter could never understand why comrade Esselwein would not sign her autograph book. After all, they did get arrested together. It was not until later, when he appeared in court in full uniform as a Sergeant of the R.C.M.P. to testify against Tim Buck, that they gathered that the man suffered, quite obviously, from a terrible identity crisis.

Fools Rush In

A message was left for me on a weekend saying that Jack McDonald wanted to see me in his office early Monday morning.

In 1929 Jack McDonald was the national secretary of the Communist Party of Canada. A pattern maker who had been in the trade union movement for years, had been an Independent Labor Party candidate in the Ontario provincial elections in 1919 and he had become the first secretary of the Party after its establishment in 1924. He was the ideal worker-leader, whom we were prepared to admire and follow.

Handsome in a rugged way, with a pleasant Scottish burr to his voice, he was the type, it seemed to me, who should have had kind, tolerant feelings towards the young people in the ranks. Although he appeared on the verge of treating us that way, somehow or other it never came off.

Subsequent events revealed that the Young Communist League top 'active' had been antagonistic to McDonald considering his leadership of the party rightist and at the last party convention had campaigned against him and supported Tim Buck for secretary of the Party. I later recalled that I had heard Charlie Marriott and Oscar Ryan making slighting remarks at the mention of Jack McDonald's name.

No wonder he was distrustful and perfunctory!

Some of this was still in the future when I reported to his office in the early part of September 1929.

He looked me over very coldly and announced in an unkind dry voice: "You are to go to Hamilton to raise relief for the strikers at the National Steel Car plant. This is to be done through the Workers' International Relief. Make all the necessary arrangements. Do you think you can do it?"

And then he added: "Is this what you are going to wear among the strikers?"

"This" referred to a gray fall coat with a fox collar. Made for me by my brother-in-law Willie. I rejoiced in this bit of elegance.

"You are to go to Hamilton..." Did this mean that someone, or a

Fools rush in

Jack MacDonald, c. 1929

committee, at any rate not he, had made this decision and he was against it? I got the feeling that he considered me a young inexperienced girl, even flighty, judging by the fox collar and the high heels, and it was silly, perhaps even irresponsible, to treat the needs of the strikers so frivolously.

Had he said so I would have agreed with him but he didn't, so I accepted the assignment without a murmur and being much in awe of his presence, asked no questions.

I merely requested permission to change my name to that of Minnie Shelley or Rose M. Shelley. At this time, foreign-born 'agitators' were already being deported to the country of their birth, a process greatly accelerated in the Depression years to come. I had no desire to end up back in Roumania and I thought that changing my name might muddy up the trail a bit for the R.C.M.P. That, plus a bit of romanticism, catapulted Min Shelley into the strikers' ranks.

As nothing was said about my living expenses, I withdrew some money from my savings account (I had $68 saved up from my period of

The Wretched of the Earth and—Me

Maurice Spector, c. 1929

prosperity through employment) and proceeded to make my way to Hamilton.

If we were invited someplace, to speak or attend a special meeting, money might be sent by the local committee for transportation; otherwise we had to get there on our own, mostly by hitch-hiking.

Hitch-hiking was dangerous. On their way to a furniture workers' strike in Stratford, two of our female Young Communist League members had actually been raped and I once had a narrow escape from an amorous truck driver on the same road, same strike. To escape his advances I begged him to stop the truck and let me out and after he did so, he passed me, driving slowly, jeering, while I walked for miles, afraid to risk another "lift." At no time in Ontario was it ever suggested that girls travelling on Party work should not hitch-hike. Could the fellow workers driving trucks be accused, even if only by insinuation, of taking advantage of their own?

When I finally arrived in Hamilton, I rented a room at $6 a week at the home of Stanley Marriner, who was the leader of the strike, and felt established.

Fools rush in

The strike was, in the first place, a struggle against a wage cut. The regular hours in the plant were 10 hours a day and the work extended over six full days—a 60-hour week. The average wage, for the most arduous work and for the most skilled category, was in this plant of 600 workers, $24 a week. It was this rate of 40 cents an hour that management was proposing to cut and that the workers, unorganized and desperate, were fighting. So desperate were they, that they accepted help from whoever offered, in this case from the Communists. Harvey Murphy, a capable YCLer, hard-working and very devoted to the trade union movement, was accepted into the strike committee.

On September 16, Charlie Sims, the district secretary of the Party, issued a directive to Harvey Murphy to the Party in Hamilton, laying down guidelines for my activities.

```
        District Commitee, C. P. in C.

Sept. 16th/29

To Comrade H. Murphy
Fox, Sec. Hamilton CCC
and Party Fraction in CLDL

Comrades,
```

The DEC has appointed Comrade M. Shelley to organize Party activities in connection with the Relief Campaign for the Steel Car strike. She will immediately commence work on the following line.

1.) In collaboration with the Hamilton CCC of the Party, and the C.C.C. of the C.L.D.L., she will draft a plan for a house to house collection. All Party and YCL members will participate in this collection, which should take place at once. (Suggest to begin on Thursday. Strikers can be also got to collect thru the Strike Committee.) Lists (possibly in the various languages will be prepared by Comrade Duhany,) can be got out by the Hungarian comrades.

The Wretched of the Earth and—Me

2.) Hamilton CCC secretary will call a special membership meeting at once to arrange for the above plan.

3.) Until CLDL Relief Committee can be organized all finance raised will be administered by the Strike Committee as today, Re the Conference for Relief it is essential that speakers go to the various organizations appealed to, therefore comrade Shelley with the Hamilton comrades will do everything possible to get a list of speakers (Strikers must be included) and arrange to secure the floor at the various meetings.

Comrades this is an important task of our Party, so comrade Shelley must receive all support and co-operation from the entire party & League membership.

Your comrade,

District Secretary

Charlie Sims.

Charlie Sims.

(Ontario Archives 10C-2277)

However, I was not sent a copy, so I proceeded on my own, in all directions at once.

I had to have a "committee"—I could not do it alone. To start with, I searched for the members of the Workers International Relief. It had not yet been set up, nor could I find the Canadian Labor Defense League. It was not yet in existence in Hamilton. (I had been referred to these two bodies for help.)

The road to setting up a committee of this sort was long and difficult. Many things had to be done first, preferably before the strike started.

I was to go to the mass organizations and ask for volunteers, having to wait for the meetings to take place first—some of them met only twice monthly—get a list of these organizations, find out where and when they met, approach their executive committees, preferably beforehand, all of this not necessarily in that order.

The strike could be over by the time such a body could even pass its first motion.

"To heck with it," I said in the genteel 1929 jargon. "I'll start by myself."

First of all we had to raise money so that strike relief could be instituted, at once.

The trade unions, that's where the money was. Someone pointed out to me where all these august bodies met and, accompanied by a male striker, I began, night after night, to knock at their doors.

"We represent the strikers at the National Steel car plant. They are fighting a wage cut. Let's face it. Today it is them. Tomorrow it may be you. We need help."

I sure did not look like a steel worker, not even a female one in my elegant gray coat with the fox collar, and they looked at me in astonishment. But we had credentials signed by Stanley Marriner and what could they do?

Craft unions all, they recognized the necessity of helping when the unorganized wanted a union and were fighting a wage cut to boot.

I briefly recounted what was going on and walked away with the not inconsiderable sum of $50 and $75 from each meeting, not as a collection but money voted from the treasury. Best of all was the applause. I hadn't known I could "speak."

"If they didn't keep us waiting too long while they're discussing the matter, we could address two meetings in one evening," I said to my partner, agog with the success of it all. I did not mind the late hours, often getting back to my room after midnight.

I was up at sunrise the next morning as Harvey Murphy had issued an order that all women had to appear on the picket line each morning to boost morale.

"You'll meet some of the women on the picket line. Try and get them to join the relief committee," said Murphy.

The rest of the day I had to myself.

Press releases highlighting the strike had to be sent out immediately across Canada.

I wrote to my skeptical comrade Jack McDonald:

The Wretched of the Earth and—Me

Strikers Relief
STRIKERS RELIEF COMMITTEE
927 Barton St. East
Hamilton, Ont, Oct, 7 1929

J. McDonald,
Secretary C.P.C.
163 1/2 Church St. Toronto.

Dear Comrade,
In connection with the national campaign being launched by the WIR of Hamilton for relief of steel Car Strikers, it is neccessary for me to have the following:
  1. A list of subscribers to each of the following: Canadian Labor Monthly, Worker, Vaupas, Ukrainian Labor News, Kamf, Mankas, .
  2. Names and addresses of all communist Party organizations. (DEC's LEC's and units)
  3. All possible names and addresses of all fraternal, cultural etc working class organizations, such as ULFTA, Finnish-Organization, CLDL, Jewish Labor Leagues, Womans Labor Leagues etc
  4. Names and addresses of individual connections.

I hope you will see your way clear to furnish this information to me as soon as possible,

Comradely yours,

(Author collection)

To this astonishing and brash request McDonald replied promptly and co-operatively but signed the letter with a rubber stamp:

Communist Party of Canada

Room 15, Athena Building
163 1/2 Church Street
Toronto 2 Canada

R.M.Shelley
927 Barton St. E.
Hamilton, Ont.

Dear Comrade Shelley,

Your request in your letter of 7th inst is quite a tall order.
We are of the opinion that the better course to pursue in this regard is to send a bundle of your bulletins or appeals to the respective papers, or organizations, with the request that they be mailed to their membership. We believe that this will be done, if you send an accompanying letter with the material.
The address of the Worker you know. Also Vapaus (Bocx 69, Sudbury) Ukrainian Labor News, Ukr Labor Temple, Pritchard and McGregor Sts. Winnipeg,

Comradely yours

J MacDonald

Secy.   (Author Collection)

The Wretched of the Earth and—Me

Greatly encouraged, I sat down at my rented typewriter and issued appeals for money in all directions, winging press releases to all corners of the country. These were strictly for the left press. Fearing that they would misinterpret or ignore our side, the local papers were left strictly alone and they left us alone, never sending a reporter to interview anyone or to take photographs of the picket line and published little, if anything, of the reasons for the strike.

I knew that somewhere I could find a sympathetic reporter but then the steel industry regarded itself as providing the bread and butter of a large section of the population of Hamilton, newspaper editors and reporters included, and I felt it useless to try. Besides, I had no time.

The strikers were not wrong in accepting the help offered them from the left. In no time at all, there were indefatigable little ants running all over, gathering, popularizing, sending clothes, money or encouragement and collecting funds by quarters and 50-cent pieces on the collection lists issued by the Strikers Relief Committee.

Comrade Bella Herzog has been authorized by the Striker's Relief Committee to collect relief funds for the National Steel Car Strikers.

M. Shelley
Striker's Relief Committee.

Name	Address	Amt
H Clairmont	219 Lippincott Ave	25.
Talamoina, Fred	St John Street	50.
Harris, Frederick	Kensington St	50.
Mathilde Buchnor	"	50.
Cirril Lipski	"	50.
Otto Buchenkhorner	Beverley Hr	50.

(Author's Collection)

Some people drew up their own collection lists and sent them in, as did Nick Lobus in Shawinigan Falls, Que., with the $7.00 donated by six well wishers and $1 donated by two others at 50 cents each.

Things were not always a roaring success. Becky Buhay wrote from

Windsor: "Dear Minnie: The house-to-house collection was a flop... I am sending just twenty-two dollars and thirty-five cents, that's all up to now.... There is quite a bit of clothes and groceries but the question is how to send it.... Could anyone come up with a car or truck?"

Murdock Clarke wrote from Cape Breton:

I told the miners that I knew you personally, and the strike was a real one etc. pointed out reasons for strike and the role of the A.F. of L. etc. To tell the truth I couldn't ever remember seeing you but if anybody asks 'you know me well.'

Were you at the League Convention when I was there? To make a long story short, after a hot debate the amendment of the reactionaries to put the question in the 'graveyard' was overwhelmingly defeated and the motion to send $50.00 and a letter accompanying it explaining that the local was with the Hamilton strikers up to the hilt was almost carried unanimously.

(Author Collection)

Poor Murdock.

I had forgotten to keep him informed as to gyrations regarding my name. I signed my accompanying letter to him "Minnie Davis," omitting to explain the "Shelley" part.

The strike dragged on.

A store was rented for $25 a month at 927 Barton Street East to be the strikers and relief headquarters and I opened a bank account. However, I had problems of my own:

The Wretched of the Earth and—Me

Chas. Sims
District Organizer #3 C.P.C.

Dear Charlie:

Please send me some money as I need some very badly and have run out of mine completely.
Thanks.

R. Minnie Shelley

522 Cannon St. E., Hamilton.

No one had suggested that I could put myself on some salary from the relief committee, so I waited for money from the Party District Office, which was always broke. I paid Stanley Marriner $6.00 a week for the room—board was not included. Apparently, Charlie Sims sent me $2.00

In the meantime, my love affair with the trade unions cooled off and petered out. Early in October, Sam Lawrence, a prominent local trade union leader, addressed the Hamilton Trades and Labor Council and as a result of his speech it was decided to refuse further requests for financial assistance to the strike. Statements were made that the strike was Communist-led and the Communist press (*The Worker*) had referred to the local AF of L leaders as fakers and traitors.

"They have their nerve coming to us and asking for money," said Sam Lawrence with some justification.

After this event, the Relief Committee found most union doors closed, except for an odd one and no more money was voted for strikers' aid. At the same time the local press became vocal and gloatingly, I thought, printed such tit-bits as:

REFUSE MONEY TO STRIKERS
and
KLANSMEN GATHER AT DEMONSTRATION

(*Hamilton Spectator*).

Fools Rush In

When the Klansmen paraded, the strike was just into its fourth week and if those behind the Klan parade considered that burning crosses would intimidate the workers, they were right. They frightened some, but it also made many strikers angry and the result was a draw.

There were also charges that relief was not distributed fairly. In my Jimmy Higgins role I had nothing to do with distribution, my job was to keep relief coming in. Relief was handled by the Strike Committee, which made the decisions as to whom relief was to be given. Relief, apparently, was to be a weapon to encourage those who were most active in the strike and to activate laggards (handing out relief to those on the picket line) but I knew nothing of this until years after.

I complained to Murphy about the articles in *The Worker*.

"All I can say to *The Worker* is thanks for the help...

Couldn't we have handled this more diplomatically... calling them names at this time?... We have no other place to go for money."

"Organize a committee, Minnie. Get suggestions. New ideas."

I did not need any more new ideas. I had enough of my own and getting another committee together (somehow I did not quite adhere to the belief in the magical power of committees) was one more job too many. But I did run around for a few days canvassing for volunteers.

By this time my inexhaustible enthusiasm ran ahead of my physical endurance and I finally went to a meeting of the strike committee, which met every day, to make a report on my work (they had never requested this) and to ask for help. They kept me waiting. One hour went by; two hours went by.

"They are not going to have time for you, they are not going to make time for you," I warned myself.

The Committee knew I was there waiting.

Eventually, P. Wilkinson, the union's vice-president, emerged. He didn't ask me in, but inquired derisively if this was not too late for the "skinny little girl" to be up. I was hungry and very tired. This was too much and I started to cry. Great sobs shook me, and although I was ashamed of it, I could not stop. Wilkinson sent Harvey Murphy out, who calmed me down somewhat, and I walked home wearily to my room in the Marriner household, where my last week's rent was still unpaid.

I never made a report to the strike committee, but whenever Wilkinson saw me afterwards, he mockingly stifled sobs in recognition of his understanding that a woman is still only a woman after all.

The Wretched of the Earth and—Me

On October 16th, the Striker's Relief Committee issued a financial statement showing that $2042.00 was collected, of which $1875.00 went to strike relief, $30.00 for rent, and $135.00 for printing, postage, carfare and stationary. Balance on hand was 73 cents.

On Friday October 18th, the strike at the National Steel car plant was called off. I issued one more communique to the 'press.'

"...through the pressureof six weeks of strike the company was forced to raise rates amounting to 15c. an hour on day rates...The splendid response made it possible for the Relief Committee to give $3.00 and $5.00 a week to the strikers... at the same time the union is appealing for aid for the blacklisted men numbering 200...Please convey this message from the men who were on strike to the workers who have helped us... with greetings of working-class solidarity, R. M. Shelley, Sercretary
Strike Relief Committee

In three days a Strikers' Relief Conference actually took place. Its session was very brief:

Motion: (Wornick)
"That support be given to the blacklisted men out of funds left, and if any more funds come in to be paid over to the union to be used for the same purpose." Carried unanimously.

My assignment was over.

Once more I hitch-hiked back to Toronto.

A week later, a letter was forwarded to me, containing kind words and regrets:

```
        The Province of Ontario Savings Office
              Parliament Buildings
                    Toronto

Nov.5/29
Miss R.M. Shelley
256 Balmoral Ave. N.
Hamilton

Dear Miss Shelley:

It is with regret that I see, from the reports
```

reaching me this morning that you have closed your account with us.
Have we been at fault in any way?

I sincerely hope that your action is not due to any lack of courtesy and attention
Sincerely Yours,

R Denisson
Director.

Isms or the impure in thought

"Your wife is a Trotskyist. How can you...well... fraternize with her?"
"Easy! You see, all day I work. At night, well, we don't talk much..."

Human beings have an illimitable fund of devotion. Happy and well-adjusted are they who find a worth-while shrine at which to lay their loyalty, their greatest efforts and around which to entwine their hopes and dreams.

My shrine was 'the movement' but we had to be young and brave and strong to follow all its precepts and adjust to its turnings, twistings and often irrational demands.

I tried very hard to become 'politicized.'

I read *What Is To Be Done* by Lenin, an important work dealing with organization and discipline and attacking a German social democrat called Bernstein. Bernstein had apparently rejected the theory of the class struggle as envisioned by Karl Marx and originated and propounded 'revisionism,' the theory of achieving socialism by peaceful means by evolution, writes Ivan Avakumovic in *The Communist Party in Canada*.

I didn't understand most of it but I laboured under the realization and fear that in a revolutionary situation, as happened in Russia in 1917, following Bernstein or following Lenin might make the difference between creating a "bourgeois democracy" or a "Soviet Republic" and apparently I preferred a Soviet Republic. One had to be well informed on theory because one had to be prepared to lead and although I was young and inexperienced, I was prepared not to shirk my duty and my destiny.

I struggled through *The History of the Communist Party of the Soviet Union* and, while travelling to work on the streetcar, I read INPRECOR (International Press Correspondence), an onionskin tabloid in small print, published abroad, we understood, by a committee of the Communist International and dealing with world-wide social and political problems. Again, I found it difficult to become interested and involved in the agrarian situation in Hyderabad or the progress and development of hydro-electric power in the area of the Caspian Sea.

Isms or the impure in thought

Looking around at the other Canadians on the streetcar, I could not but speculate on whither I was going, why and will I like it if I ever got there? I felt my isolation from the others, my estrangement. Was I ahead of the crowd, in the rear, or an oddball on the fringe?

On the whole, we proceeded with our day-to-day work, contacting the 'masses' and paying cursory attention to the ideological struggles in the Party. The theoretical pot was always bubbling and sometimes roiling and boiling and running over, as it did very shortly after I joined the Young Communist League.

In 1928 we heard the more politicized members of the YCL— Charlie Marriott, Leslie Morris, Oscar Ryan—discussing the possible adherence of Maurice Spector to the Trotskyist camp. Maurice Spector was the chairman of the Party, a member of the Executive Committee of the Communist International elected at the 6th Congress and a very clever man and a gifted theoretician.

We new members quickly learned the glib explanation of Trotskyite theories. The building of socialism in one country was impossible, said Leon Trotsky; the Soviet Union must mark time until the "permanent revolution" brought about changes in the Western countries first.

Trotsky and his followers, such as Bukharin (a prominent Russian theoretician, a co-worker of Lenin's and a leader of the Russian revolution), were accused of fomenting opposition by the *kulaks* (the more prosperous peasants) to collectivization, the murder of party leaders, for example Sergei Kirov, destructive sabotage, etc. (Tim Buck, *Thirty Years*)

More sinister yet, and laying the groundwork for the dreadful trials of the founders of the Communist Party who carried through the Russian revolution, were the charges that the Trotskyites turned to the path of counter-revolution plotting to overthrow the government. It was claimed that the Trotskyites offered to "agree to the Japanese seizure of the eastern Maritime provinces and German seizure of the Ukraine ... in payment for military assistance to them in overthrowing Soviet power" (Tim Buck, *Thirty Years*)

Reports were given to the membership of the Canadian Party, which demonstrated beyond a doubt that following Trotsky would lead to the liquidation of socialism in the Soviet Union. All the pertinent books were searched, the pronouncements of Lenin against Trotsky produced and Stalin became the man of iron fighting for socialism against the revisionism of Trotsky.

The Wretched of the Earth and—Me

At all-night meetings reports were given and astounding revelations brought to light. Maurice Spector, Jay Lovestone in the U.S.A. and even Jack McDonald, the secretary of the Party, were shown to be out and out Trotskyite renegades. Devoted, sincere Communists who had been in the party since its founding and 'left socialists' before that were deeply shocked to hear beloved and respected leaders called "traitors" and worse and agonized as to which was the right road to follow.

Following the 'right line' or the 'wrong line' seemed a matter of life and death. Following Trotsky could be held against you for the rest of your existence; it could mean the end of your very life under certain revolutionary situations.

A whole cabal of charges and counter-charges were unleashed. *The Worker* ran continual long articles and published statement upon statement:

> STATEMENT OF THE POLCOM OF C.P.
> of C. ON THE TORONTO MEMBERSHIP
> VOTE ON TROTSKYISM
>
> 99% of the Toronto membership of the C.P. have taken a clear definite stand against Trotskyism and for the expulsion of Morris Spector.... Nevertheless, there is a small number of honest revolutionaries in Toronto who have vacillated on the question.... Such honest comrades will be given a period of six months probation in which to confirm their party loyalty. The Party, however, must be purged of all anti-party elements....
>
> The Polcom takes this opportunity of reaffirming its statement that within the party the widest democracy prevails for Party views and honest proletarian self-criticism. But there will be no toleration for anti-party views....
>
> The Polcom reaffirms its line of struggle on two fronts; against Trotskyism on one hand and against the main danger of the present period, the danger from the right. This in no sense means a centrist policy but a clear Leninist policy against the 'left' phrases of the Trotskyists and right opportunism.
>
> —*The Worker*, January 26, 1929.
> Editor: Mike Buhay, (subsequently expelled for Trotskyism.)

Isms or the impure in thought

And then the expulsions and then 'purgings' began.:

> The following members have been expelled from the C.P of Canada: M. Bergstein, D. Quarter, J. (Jimmy) Blugerman, D. Quarter, Z. Queller, W. Bosovich, Bill Chainak, H. Popper.
> —*The Worker,* January 26, 1929

> Expelled from the Party were Fred Peel, Bill Moriarty, R. Shoesmith, Ahlquist and A. Vaara (editor of the Finnish *Vaupas*) and Mike Buhay editor of *The Worker*.

These lists were published every week and we read them in horror. We felt at the crossroads. Which way to go? Former comrades, now Trotskyists, frightened us fresh young Communists by boldly stating that there is no socialism in the Soviet Union, what is in existence there is STATE CAPITALISM, therefore it is justifiable to overthrow the Soviet Government.

That did it. With all our hearts we believed socialism was being built in the Soviet Union, we knew it was so and anyone who denied it was a traitor. After that it was easy to vote for the expulsions, to join in ridicule and in indignation against the Lovestone-ite "exceptionalists" who believed in the the theory that American capitalism was so strong that it would avoid the periodic economic recessions afflicting other countries, and Trotskyite "opportunism."

It was at this time that we were tearing each other to shreds that I first learned that "self-criticism" was nothing but an opportunity to commit "hara kiri." There was nothing friendly about this self-criticism, nor was it constructive. It was a weapon for self-destruction.

Persons who were expelled as Trotskyists were ostracized. We didn't talk to them, we didn't fraternize; husbands lost wives and girls their boyfriends and neighbours turned icy when meeting a former dear friend on the street. Very few didn't take it so seriously. One man refused to leave his wife.

"But how can you fraternize with her, how evan you talk to her?" he was asked.

"Well," he replied with a wee smile, "you see, all day I go to work and at night in the dark, we don't talk much...."

The Wretched of the Earth and—Me

And then there was the matter of what happened to Harry.

Perhaps it was during the Trotskyite expulsions that we began being afraid of infection by *bourgeois* ideas.

To announce that you had an individual theory which you wanted to present to a district committee for consideration, as Harry Fistell did in Toronto, was like announcing that you had the plague. Everyone, terrified of being infected, drew back in horror.

Harry Fistell, who had original ideas on how the Party should function in the field of *bourgeois* culture, the role of the party in the fight for peace and specific ideas on election campaigns, was severely examined, cross-examined, bullied, intimidated and, after months of being tried and diagnosed, was finally cast out of the Party, never to be re-admitted.

Anyone of us who harbored non-conformist theories on how matters could be improved in the functioning of the Party only had to recall the cruel fate of Harry Fistell to immediately resolve to toe the line without deviating one inch one way or the other, forevermore.

To be truly snow white, clean, Communist-minded, we tried not to mingle with other people, non-Communists that is, for we might get infected with impure, capitalist thoughts.

I, for one, was too brave in exposing myself to non-orthodox influences.

Other people suffered from my rashness, including Jerry Rosen.

Invited to visit Haekel Faessler, a sculptor who had a studio on Grenville Street, I asked Jerry to come along. Haekel was a neighbour at the office of the *Young Comrade*, the monthly publication of the Young Pioneers that I edited. He had Communist and non-Communist friends and accepted each on his or her own worth as an individual human being.

The appointed evening came and I met Jerry on Grenville Street in front of the building. He was twitching, uneasy. He didn't like the street. "Who lives here? What kind of a place is it?"

"It's alright, they're nice people, come and see. The Young Pioneers has its headquarters here."

Inside, the studio was inviting. Paintings on the wall, a fire in the grate, wine on the table. He looked around, unhappy at everything he saw, like a Talmudic scholar in a message parlour.

I took some wine, lit a cigarette, left him alone. He did not participate in the conversation, eyed abstract paintings on the wall with distaste, sat down, got up again and twitched some more.

Isms or the impure in thought

"Oh boy, have I ever fallen in," he muttered in an aside to me in Yiddish, indicating he had fallen amongst worse than thieves.

He had wandered into unorthodox, impure surroundings where non-Communist utterances might be voiced at any moment, defiling and besmirching him entirely. He found nothing to approve of. Participating in the conversation would indicate acceptance of the non-conformist bohemian life style of those present.

We left shortly after. I sensed his disapproval. Nothing was said but at the corner of Yonge and Greenville we parted and he went his way and I went mine.

General Draper's Iron Heel

Neither this government nor any other government that I am a member of will ever grant unemployment insurance. We will not put a premium on idleness or put our people on the dole.

—R. B. Bennett, Conservative Prime Minister of Canada, to a twenty-four man delegation presenting a petition for unemployment insurance signed by 100,000 people, sponsored by the Workers Unity League

Without the dole people starved and if they would not starve in silence, Prime Minister Bennett, in a speech to the Ontario Conservative Association, promised *the iron heel of ruthlessness would be used.* Toronto, ever faithfully Tory, followed the party line and to equip itself with an iron heel turned to the military for its chief of police. General Draper, in turn, appointed one Detective William Nursey as head of the newly-formed 'Red Squad.' Nursey, with two assistants, Mann and Simpson, formed a formidable trio, tough and frightful to us all. Tall, husky, well-fed and well-dressed (at least they wore overcoats and hats), they would be the uninvited guests at every meeting, every concert, every public gathering.

One look at the three slowly and menacingly advancing down an aisle and the old-timers would turn pale, while the newly-joined and 'sympathizers' with jobs and relatives to protect would surreptitiously look around for the nearest exit.

The harassment would extend from having the 'Red Squad' walk into offices and pick up and examine documents to refusing a Finnish restaurant a license because "reds ate there."

One of the earliest activities of the Communist movement in Toronto was that of taking its programme to the people by the time-honored means of street-corner meetings. It was cheap, it dispensed with the hiring of a hall and a crowd could always be counted on, be it only 10 or 12 people.

We had favorite spots. One of the earliest was at Pacific and Dundas

General Draper's iron heel

Streets, then we progressed to Soho and Queen and finally to Albert and Yonge. However, Albert and Yonge on Sunday evenings was always pre-empted by revivalists, so we moved west one block to James and Albert, behind Eaton's store, a lonely, unfrequented spot on weekends.

Even so, these gatherings were dispersed and the speakers arrested, as were Tim Buck, Oscar Ryan, Harvey Murphy, Stewart Smith, Lillian Himmelfarb, J.B. Salsberg, Sam Langley, and Becky Buhay.

Although heavy charges were dangled over the speakers' heads—of illegal assembly, disorderly conduct and sedition—the charges against most of those arrested actually were dismissed by reasonable judges and only a small percentage were sent down to the jail farm for 30 days.

It was different with the advent of the rule of General Draper.

An overall blanket of interdiction was laid on. Local owners of public halls were prohibited from renting their premises for "Communist meetings" on pain of having their licenses revoked, all meetings were to take place in "English only," even if 100% of the audience was Bulgarian or Croatian, and any speaker who wandered off from English into another language was dragged off the platform. There was the instance of one Albert Graves, who was arrested for speaking in French.

Most painful blow of all, every street-corner meeting was dispersed almost immediately by mounted police.

However, as the authorities were naturally not advised in advance as to where the meetings were going to be held, the police had the difficult and irritating task of running from one brush fire to the other in their efforts to extinguish the red flames. Did they mind? Without seeming to ever tire or flag in effort, General Draper and his men of the Red Squad carried out zestfully their mandate of crushing all 'Red' activity with an iron heel. No hour was too late, no place was sacrosanct.

The Worker complained bitterly and angrily every week:

> Protest against the arrest of 6 workers in the Free Speech fight. George Andrews, Joe Farbey, Sam Langley, Oscar Ryan, Stewart Smith Pat O'Sullivan— March 8, 1931

> On June 9th, detectives raided houses of members of various organizations, intimidating the women they found at home. They followed this up by raiding the

The Wretched of the Earth and—Me

> Ukrainian Labor Temple at 300 Bathurst Street, where a meeting of unemployed was in progress. They dispersed the crowd and arrested two people who were later released.
>
> Draper's thugs have been at their usual tricks of picking up workers and intimidating them. On June 1, Joe Carey was arrested, threatened, roughly used and told to leave town. —Saturday, June 20, 1931.

On the same day, while delivering copies of *The Worker* to newsstands, a Mr. Wilson was "set upon by detectives, taken to a police station, beaten, threatened, searched and then released."

> ... Detectives raided the premises of the Workers' Sports Association, forced locks, opened doors and searched everything. A member who happened to come in while this was going on and saw them handling the membership lists was threatened by the detectives and roughly ordered out.
>
> ... Joe Forkin, an Alderman from Ward 3 in the Winnipeg City Council was arrested, questioned, threatened and ordered to leave town.
>
> ...of six persons who were arrested at a meeting on May Day in Toronto, one was released and five were held over for trial in a higher court in the Fall assizes, the charges of "wounding" being changed to that of "unlawful assembly."

Finally, in August 1931 the authorities decided that perhaps the heart of the matter was the left-wing press and they went straight for it:

> Following a raid by police on the Model Printing and the removal of type and confiscation of leaflets, a summons has been served on Tim Buck, secretary of the Communist Party of Canada, and the printer, Joe

General Draper's iron heel

> Kleinstein on charges of: Willfully, knowingly publishing or causing to be published false news or tales, thereby injury or mischief is likely to be occasioned to public interest— *The Worker*, Saturday, August 1, 1931.

Denied the street corners, we boldly took to Queen's Park, where the bandshell formed a most suitable stand for speakers. Permission to hold meetings being denied, we insisted on our right to these gatherings—all seemingly destined to be broken up. The result was a weekly confrontation, each side deploying its forces to the best of its abilities and resources.

At Queen's Park every Saturday afternoon, a regular military formation met the eye. The bandshell, where the speaker was to hold forth, was ringed by a cordon of Toronto's finest (not one of them under six feet tall), the second line was the motorcycle brigade and finally, and most terrifying of all, the mounted police. We feared them the most. They actually did not ride their mounts directly into the crowd as we, with Cossacks in mind, feared but used the horses' flanks to move us about, a crowd-control tactic. However, we could not be entirely sure that they would not ride over us, or into us. We discussed how to deal with the horses.

"Have little bags of black pepper," someone suggested, "and throw the pepper into the horses' eyes." Mercifully, that was rejected.

Then came our forces, an unorganized fluid crowd, supporters, sympathizers and those who were there only for the fun. In this mob were the dauntless few determined to reach the bandshell and hold the meeting.

Sometimes, aided by a diversion, a speaker would actually reach the stand, heroically threading his way through three rings of defence, followed by no one at all, only to be hauled off immediately and thrown into the paddy wagon which was always there, waiting.

We reaped a harvest of sympathy.

Many Toronto people, not necessarily interested in the politics involved, began to admire the hard-fighting 'reds' and the appearance of mounted police riding into crowds in front of the very parliament of the people did not sit too well with those used to the British way of free speech. Even the local press acted with indignation when a University of

The Wretched of the Earth and—Me

Toronto professor, absent-mindedly crossing the park, became embroiled in the fray, was roughened up and arrested while protesting, in vain, his lack of interest in reaching the bandstand.

The meetings grew in fierceness and size, at one time as many as 10,000 milling about and participating in the goings on.

All that summer of 1931, the work at the Toronto Jail Farm was efficiently and vigorously performed by various shifts of the Toronto 'red' active, all in for 30 days at the time. This game of cops and reds lasted until winter came and in the meantime more than punctuated our way of life.

"I'll see you in Queen's Park on Saturday" was the standard adieu and for many citizens going down to the park to see the fights provided a little dangerous amusement—"it's a sort of a tag," some explained, "available for free."

Even though they did not get to address the crowd, only the very best speakers were selected for Queen's Park and it was a much-sought-after honour.

However, we inexperienced YCL-ers and girls (whose voices did not carry too well in the open air) did get our chance every now and then at street-corner meetings that we still tried to hold even for a short time until the police arrived.

I was appointed to be speaker at one such meeting organized by the Young Communist League on a Sunday evening at James and Albert Streets, right outside Eaton's store.

I had been carrying on for about 10 minutes in my thin, rather squeaky voice when a young policeman turned up.

"Do you have a permit, lady?" he shouted at me.

I took the situation in. He was alone and obviously a rookie.

"The policeman," I cheekily explained to the crowd, "wants to know if I have a permit. Since when does a lady need a permit to talk?"

The crowd laughed, the policeman made a lunge for me and I shinnied up a lamp post. About two feet up there was a trim on the metal that provided me with a hold. Hugging the post with one arm, I surveyed the crowd and the policeman. Judging my position favourable, and in the best tradition of a Rosa Luxembourg, a Krupskaya or, best of all, a Sylvia Pankhurst, I continued to orate in my squeaky voice, attracting even more people from my unlikely stance. Of course, this was a challenge to the officer, who continued to advance, somewhat impeded

General Draper's iron heel

by a hostile crowd. He made a lunge for me and I climbed a little higher. He tried again and managed to pull at some underthings.

A half slip came down and became visible. There was a hushed sound. "Shame," intoned the crowd and someone yelled: "Leave the little girl alone." The policeman, red-faced and confused, recognizing a draw, withdrew, covering his retreat by taking out his report book and scribbling away.

It was a great victory for our side and while later Tim Buck reported it to an international gathering as an example of courage among the youth, I was actually not proud of myself. With my unfortunate tendency of trying to see both sides of a situation, I felt that the medal for courage, if any, should go to the policeman, who advanced against odds into hostile territory to do a job he was hired for. What if he had had to report that a mere slip of a girl had given him the slip? Well, jobs were hard to get in the Depression and the police, too, are part of the working class.

The free speech meetings were held in the evenings or on Saturday afternoons, but as the Depression advanced and greater numbers were unemployed, we all began to spend more time helping the jobless to set up associations, find headquarters and organize delegations to the authorities. The single men asked for relief and the right to remain in the city rather than be shipped off to work camps.

Working full time at this, without being paid, I made continual attempts to get work. To my surprise, I was hired as an assistant bookkeeper by a wholesale fish firm on King Street East, not far from the St. Lawrence Market.

However, my heart belonged to the Single Unemployed Association, which I had helped organize and which had its headquarters at 650 Bay Street. In Toronto at that time, single men or women when unemployed were not entitled to relief or assistance of any sort, City Hall hoping that if parents could not support them they would drift away. Many did, 'riding the rods' even to Vancouver, much to the aggravation of the government of British Columbia, that province being favored by the single unemployed as a good place to spend the winter.

Shortly after I commenced working once more, the Single Unemployed Association of Toronto called a public meeting in front of City Hall for noon hour. They were asking for relief at the modest rate of $3 a week for single persons and, of course, for unemployment insurance.

The Wretched of the Earth and—Me

I was working now, but I had helped them during an evening meeting to draw up their demands and I knew some of the single young men. (We could not get unemployed girls to join up. They were too timid to admit publicly to being unemployed and found the associations, predominantly male, too rough and uncongenial.)

The meeting was called for 12 o'clock. How to get there? I asked permission to leave 15 minutes before noon and proceeded to take the streetcar to the demonstration. I arrived, I demonstrated, there were scuffles and in the melee I was pounced upon by the police and arrested.

This I had not anticipated.

I was terrified! I had to get back to work! I didn't want to lose my job. I Loved my job!

Someone dragged me into one of the offices of City Hall and deposited me in front of the desk of one of the 'terrible three'— probably Detective Mann, judging by the square, black moustache. He paid no attention to me for about 20 minutes.

"Why doesn't a pretty girl like you get married and settle down?" he then queried in a smooth, kind voice.

I was stymied but replied mechanically. "Oh, I've heard all that stuff before," probably thinking of my mother.

Whereupon he turned terrible and frightened me properly, saying we were scum, I was scum, we were bums, indigents, red rabble, verminous foreigners, we were dung, thugs and I can go now. I almost didn't hear the last. I was trying to close my ears to the tongue-lashing and had to be ushered out by the attending officer.

Had Detective Mann but known it, this dressing-down was very effective. I had a need for people's approval and this massive, deeply abusive tirade really crushed me.

I rushed out and jumped on a streetcar. Oh, those lovely, friendly Toronto streetcars!

I arrived back at the office pale, breathless, but only one hour late and was astonished to note that everything was the same. I caught the admonitory but good-natured look and finger wag of the office manager, slipped into my swivel chair and sank back into the warm and comforting routine of accounts receivable.

Jobless again

Anne telephoned asking to borrow my references.

"I have applied for a job and they want me to come for an interview. I need you to do me a favor...."

My references were superior to hers, they bespoke of a better bookkeeper, longer experience and were issued by three fairly reputable firms. I was impressed with them myself, every time I read their highly encouraging contents. With such splendid recommendations, how could I still be unemployed? In addition, my surname was Davis, hers was Kohen, and when it came to getting employment in 1930, it was better not to be named Kohen. Jobs were extremely hard to get and an innocent bit of fraud for a very good cause was acceptable.

The best references got the job, provided that the applicant was also intelligent, personable and astonishingly pretty.

It worked! With her good looks and my papers, Anne was hired by a well-known manufacturer of hot-water bottles.

An impish fate, however, was to punish us for our deception. A few weeks after she started work, Anne telephoned in great agitation. "Minnie, would you like a job for a few weeks? Our stenographer was taken ill and we need a temporary replacement."

Would I? I had been unemployed for months, was completely penniless and felt guilty about living at home without paying the usual 'board' —$7 a week now. I rushed down and on Anne's recommendation, "Miss Martin" was hired, without references.

Then a gargantuan problem of "Who am I?" arose. When "Miss Davis" was called, I answered. Then Anne replied. Next time "Miss Davis" was summoned, no one stirred. "Miss Martin" was so slow in responding to her name that Anne had to agree to the kind suggestion of Mr. Sills, the office manager, that "Miss Martin" was a little hard of hearing if not actually a "little slow," meaning retarded.

The money, however, coming in every week was very welcome and when Mr. Sills finally had to terminate my employment with the return of his own stenographer, I was given an extra week's salary, an unheard of generosity in those days.

The Wretched of the Earth and—Me

Once more I was unemployed and a few weeks of paying for room and board left me penniless again.

It was the winter of 1930. There was no aid for single people. At any rate, I could not have accepted such help. My family would have disapproved and found it shameful. All I wanted was a job. These were from hard-to-get to non-existent, but I persisted.

I recalled earlier days in the '20s when I was fifteen and unemployed and I could go from factory to factory asking for work.

Now, as an office worker I could no longer do that but had to rely on the HELP WANTED-FEMALE columns of the daily newspapers.

This entailed a strict routine. The evening newspapers were available at 11 o'clock in the morning. By that hour, I was on Melinda Street, every day, waiting for the paper to come out, the favorite for jobs being *The Evening Telegram*. Dozens of people were hanging around, waiting. When the paper finally appeared, I hurriedly threw the boy a nickel, snatched a copy and then and there, on the street, quickly perused the HELP WANTED—FEMALE columns. If there was an advertisement that sounded at all promising, I jumped on a streetcar and rushed away, hoping to get an interview.

Very often, arriving tired and breathless I would find that there were dozens already ahead of me. Most often I was told the "job has been taken" as soon as I arrived, or a sign would be put up coldly stating: "Position has been filled." Sometimes I would get as far as an interview and leave behind a completed application form, which would be the end of the matter.

Having spent a nickel on the paper and seven cents carfare to chase a phantom job, I would trudge home on foot, thoroughly chilled and tired.

It was always cold that winter, a deep, penetrating Toronto cold, or it would snow and the grey slush under my feet matched the all-pervasive misery. When I arrived home, discouraged and weary, no one asked me how the day went. They could tell by my face. As usual, there was kindness and encouragement and my mother made me hot tea.

Still, it was embarrassing and uncomfortable living at home without paying board and I could not expect my stepfather to support me.

In addition, I was beset by a new worry. It was essential to present a good appearance when applying for an office job. My clothes were beginning to look shabby, the footwear definitely so, and there was hardly anyone from whom I could borrow (another good Depression

Jobless again

practice) who was my size (which was small and skinny—size 7).

Sometimes we talked about my job-hunting problems in the evening. "You have to know someone, someone important, to get a job these days." "You have to know someone who knows someone," said my stepfather, who considered himself a man of the world.

If I could not have a job, at least I needed more activity—something to occupy me, to fill these empty days.

I went to see Bill Kashtan, the new national secretary of the Young Communist League. "Yes, there is something you can do. You've been in Hamilton during the steel strike, you should know your way about."

Word had reached them of a wage cut of 10% at a Hamilton textile plant employing mostly young girls. Wages, prior to the cut, had been $8 and $10 for a 51-hour week.

"You go and organize them against the wage cut," he said. "Just get a little committee together from the plant and people from the trade union movement will take over from there." It didn't sound too difficult. I would be given detailed instructions, some addresses of contacts and $15 for expenses.

"But there will be no wages unless a local group agrees to help," he warned. I accepted.

Then I told my mother.

"Don't do that" she said. "They're lefties. And what kind of future is that for a young girl?"

"Mama, everybody is a leftie today. What does it matter? After all, I need something to do." She shook her head disapprovingly, said "What will become of you?" But made me some thick sandwiches when I left home early the next morning.

On a miserably wet and cold February morning, I took the streetcar to the end of the line, which was Long Branch, got off and after waiting for half-an-hour by the side of the road, hitched a ride.

It was even more miserable in Hamilton.

In a restaurant, I studied my contacts over a cup of coffee. There was a Jewish fraternal left-wing organization that met only once a month, there was a Croatian Benevolent Organization (what could they possibly do for me?), there was a Ukrainian Labor Temple Association with a good mandolin orchestra and an excellent male choir and a small Young Communist League group that had been studying *Value, Price and Profit* by Karl Marx. They had not been told of my impending arrival and might

The Wretched of the Earth and—Me

not be very helpful or even friendly. I was fascinated by all these activities but their application to my task eluded me.

At any rate, I found a Jewish family from the fraternal organization who took me in to sleep in an attic room, without charge, "for a few days."

"Well, for a week or so," said my hostess without enthusiasm.

In the next few days I investigated my contacts further, for Bill Kashtan had been very strong on their importance. I found the organizations on my list consisted of members who had a hard time making a living, many were unemployed and those who were working were terrified of losing their jobs. They didn't want a penniless girl organizer in their midst adding to their troubles. Those I called on offered no help, not even advice.

Where to begin? How to set up a committee in the largest textile plant in Hamilton without knowing anyone inside. I went down to the plant and looked in through the murky windows. Inside were girls working at long machines.

The next day I came down at noon hour, hoping to find young people hanging around on their lunch break. There was no one hanging around. I returned at quitting time.

The young employees came out in bunches, bundled up and seemingly tired and ran for the streetcars. No one stopped even to light up a cigarette.

Plainly, all they wanted was to get home as quickly as possible.

I had the wild idea of following one of them but wisely gave it up. I was beginning to realize that it was going to be difficult, perhaps even impossible to organize such a committee.

It was easier to help set up a Single Unemployed Men's Association.

On Market Square on a Saturday night I found a meeting in progress. The organizer was 'Fisher,' who had been on the relief committee with me during the Hamilton Steel car strike. I offered my assistance.

Together we drew up a leaflet that was duplicated in the office of the very same Croatian Benevolent Society that I had considered would be of no help at all. It called for a mass rally on Market Square that turned out to be a huge success and led to the organization of a Single Men's Unemployed Association.

In their enthusiasm, I was invited to sit in on their Executive Committee and things were going well but for one serious obstacle.

Jobless again

The organizer's shoes had come apart, the soles gaped and were tied to the uppers with strong string, which, however, did not keep out the slush and snow. Inquiries yielded the name of a member of the Jewish Fraternal Organization who owned a shoe store.

I took Fisher in and he was fitted with a brand new pair of shoes "for free." It was miraculous. Fisher was wildly happy.

"I haven't had a new pair of these since I worked at the plant!" Which made me feel very sad as I realized he was one of those who was blacklisted as a result of the strike. However, the committee solemnly declared that this demonstrated the results of good organizational work and of sticking together.

Encouraged, I tried to seek out the unemployed young women and see what I could do for them, for my sake as well. I was probably the neediest single unemployed woman in all of Hamilton. I had found no local group that wanted to "make itself responsible" for my upkeep. I was overstaying my welcome with the Jewish family. I would have to rent a room of my own and no one had invited me to their home for a meal, which I had counted on.

Where were the unemployed girls to be found anyways?

I soon found out. While I was hunting for them all over Hamilton, that cornerstone of the establishment, the Young Women's Christian Association had them flocking to its downtown branch in their dozens. The attraction was simple and timeless. They served tea with nice, thick slices of bread and butter every day at 11 o'clock, thus providing two meals in one—breakfast and lunch. I liked it myself. Very much! I went there every day, ate the bread and butter and tried to talk to some of the young women.

They obviously divided themselves into two categories. About half were easy-going types, looking for dates who would buy them bacon and eggs, boasted of it and offered this road out as a solution to their unemployed and hungry state.

"Come with us, Minnie" they invited. "We'll show you how to get some swell meals."

The others were ladies who held themselves aloof and complained of one thing only: The bread was cut too thick. "Who do they think we are giving us such thick slices?"

I had thought the thick slices were just great but then I came of Eastern European stock and had not had a thin bread-and-butter upbringing.

The Wretched of the Earth and—Me

Would I ever be able to understand them? I asked myself. Would I be able to lead them from this complaint about thick bread-and-butter to where they would demand from City Hall not only THIN bread-and-butter but RENT. No one had ever dared ask for money for rent before, not even the better organized Single Young Men's Unemployed Association. I ought to know what a menace the prospect of homelessness could be. I have to leave my room and have nowhere to go. I could already see the placards in my mind's eye.

> CITY FATHERS! DO YOU WANT TO
> FORCE US OUT ON THE STREETS? WE
> NEED RENT VOUCHERS

Unfortunately, the young women turning up at the 'Y' varied daily. They were vague, scared, uninterested. If only I had some funds I could hire a hall, issue a leaflet. But I had run out of money completely.

Obviously, something had to be done!

Leaving my suitcase behind, I hitch-hiked back to Toronto to get some help and advice. I went straight up to Anne's house, as I did not want my mother to see me in the shabby, discouraged state I was in. Mrs. Kohen welcomed me. It was good to take a hot bath, and sit down to a good home-cooked meal. Anne was still working for the hot bottle manufacturer, and we exchanged news.

"Seems like years since I was 'Miss Martin.' I wish I was working there now."

It was Saturday and in the evening we went to a party run by the YCL to raise funds. The party was dull but excitement awaited us on the way home.

At about 11.30, waiting on the sidewalk to cross the road at the corner of Palmerston Boulevard and Harbord Street, Anne and I were hit by one, or perhaps two, cars that had engaged in a head-on collision. She sustained a severe concussion and I a badly fractured jaw. We both regained consciousness in Western Hospital. I was able to inform the nurse about Anne's parents and even remembered her telephone number but my mother didn't know about the accident until Tuesday morning. A reporter from the *Toronto Star* had called at 188 Palmerston Avenue for a 'follow-up story' and, meaning to be kind, had brought Mama over in his car. She cried. I had a terrible time quieting her anxieties.

Jobless again

"This is what comes from hanging around with 'them.' I hope this teaches you a lesson," she said. I didn't argue. She came daily, carrying chicken soup in a glass jar.

The story in the *Toronto Star* also brought our mutual friend, Anne's office manager, Mr. Sills, visiting. Anne was unrecognizable. Her face was completely bandaged and what was visible was a bitter blue-black colour. Her nose and the rest of her face were on one level—swollen.

Mr. Sills came over to my bed.

"Is that her?" he asked. (She was in the bed next to me). I nodded miserably, wondered if he had it sorted out. The former 'Miss Davis' was really Anne Kohen and 'Miss Martin' was really Miss Davis and there just wasn't any Miss Martin at all....

He was nice enough to bring flowers for all of us—

Martin, Davis and Kohen.

Minnie in Manitoba

"It will take nine months at least for the paralysis to leave your face" was the blunt verdict of Dr. Duff, the capable and famous neurosurgeon who had repaired the break in my jaw. This was the most serious part of the injuries I had sustained during the automobile accident in which Anne and I had been involved. Fortunately the surgeon was right and the facial paralysis faded away, or almost.

My face never regained complete symmetry, leaving me with a slightly twisted smile, a disfigurement that helped in obtaining the astronomical out-of-court insurance settlement of $3,000.

When the money was finally in my hands, I was uncomfortable. I didn't know how to handle wealth. I made some funds available to my mother and step-father, who promptly added a little more and purchased a furnace for $500 and we no longer had to rely on the unreliable self-heater during the winter months. I made some donations here and there but I was too embarrassed by my new-found riches, too inexperienced at spending money to even buy myself some decent clothing. I wanted to share with the world but didn't know how.

"If the Party would ask me to donate the lot to the national office I would gladly do it and consider it a good riddance," I confessed to Anne.

Fortunately, they didn't come up with any such suggestions.

One day, watching a shabby 'unemployed' pick up a cigarette butt from the gutter, a common sight in the 1930s, I stopped him and muttered something like: "Do you mind if I give you some money for tobacco?" So embarrassed was I and so incoherent that the poor man thought I was asking him for money for cigarettes and said regretfully: "Gee, I'm sorry, I was just picking up a butt..."

I quickly pressed 50 cents in his hands and hurried on, mortified and unhappy. What right did I have to go around with money in the bank while people were picking cigarette butts out of the gutter?

My friend Anne did not feel guilty as the possessor of $2,700 that she had obtained from the insurance company for her injuries—a permanent scar on her forehead. She knew exactly what she wanted to do with it. She was aching to join her boyfriend Stewart Smith, who was attending the famous Lenin Institute. It was organized and maintained in Moscow by the Communist International for the purpose of training the activists of the various parties.

"Let's go, Minnie" she urged. "They have to give us leave of absence now and we have our own money. Let's go on a trip to Moscow."

I, perhaps foolishly, refused and she too remained in Canada. However, at the back of my mind was an offer from Charlie Marriott to come to Winnipeg, where he had been sent as Party organizer.

"If you need nursing care," he wrote, "the ULFTA (the Farmer-Labor Temple Association) have an old-peoples' home just outside Winnipeg which sometimes takes in convalescents. Perhaps I can arrange it."

I didn't need nursing care and the old-peoples' home didn't sound too idyllic but I bought my railway ticket and set off for Winnipeg.

I had never been west of Toronto; Winnipeg seemed part of the exciting Prairie Provinces where all men went for the harvest and it was the home of the 'Wobblies.' (They were the Industrial Workers of the World, an early militant trade union movement in the U.S. and Canada, particularly active in logging camps.)

Before machines displaced human hands on the farm, thousands of Canadian men, mostly young, would rush west to take in the harvest. Railroads ran Harvest Specials at one cent per mile. West for the harvest went Harvey Murphy, Trevor McGuire, Tom Burpee (before graduating in accountancy) and Charles Marriott. Harvest wages were $4 a day for stooking and $6 for thrashing, according to Tom McEwen in *The Forge Grows Red*. Four to six weeks on the Prairies would provide many a young man with a nest egg to tide him over the dread winter months of unemployment. The Depression and the misfortune of drought dried up these labour opportunities—indeed, dried up the farms, as well, and pushed thousands of farmers unto the unemployment heap.

Winnipeg had an interesting history and seemed an exciting city from what I had read.

I was aware that just a little over one hundred years ago, Winnipeg was settled by its first immigrants brought over by Thomas Douglas, Fifth Earl of Selkirk. To the victims of the Enclosures Act, plots of free land seemed like the wildest dream come true. They came, unprepared, unequipped and died in their hundreds of hardship and neglect.

The Wretched of the Earth and—Me

Nevertheless, as the entry to the West where free land was actually available to settlers, Winnipeg, in no time at all, was bursting with immigrants, particularly after the railroads opened up the Prairies. A large number of these immigrants were from Galicia (whose population was Polish and Ukrainian), which, until the War of 1914-1918 had been part of the Austro-Hungarian empire.

The Canadian government, favouring immigrants from the British Isles, settled the Galicians on rock-strewn soil, reserving the more fertile land for British immigrants. Nevertheless overcoming these difficulties, the settlers, men, women and children and mainly without animals, toiling from dawn to dusk, cleared the land, planted it and created life-sustaining homesteads.

Many did not reach the free land of the Prairies. Stopping off in Winnipeg, they found friends or relatives and stayed, getting jobs.

As the most recent wave of immigrants always do, they took on the dreariest and hardest work, digging ditches, paving streets, laying tracks and, if they were lucky, obtaining employment in the railroad yards of Fort Rouge or Transcona.

If and when there was no work in Winnipeg, there was seasonal work to be had in the bush, on the railroads or harvesting.

Nevertheless, 'the Galicians' were not really made welcome by the rest of the population, particularly those of Anglo-Saxon descent. If times were bad, it was easy enough to say that 'the foreigners' took whatever work was available and were to blame for hard times.

Jingoism and anti-foreign feeling brought sorrow and tragedy to the Ukrainians in Canada during the First World War. Many had neglected to become Canadian citizens, a difficult and unfamiliar procedure for them. As a result, thousands were interned during the war as 'Austrian subjects' in special camps in Vernon, British Columbia; Brandon, Manitoba; and in Kapuskasing, Ontario.

From the earliest times of their peopling the land, the Ukrainian workers and farmers had built their organizations and their 'halls,' calling them Ukrainian Farmer-Labour Temple Associations. Starting with the need of co-operative self-help and getting together with neighbours who had the same language and background, the organizations grew to provide sick and death benefits and act as a cushion to bad times and misfortune. Mutual aid, co-operatives and newspapers came into existence.

A rich cultural life, starting even with teaching adults arithmetic, geography and to read and write, created in the left-wing Ukrainians a cultured, educated and politically aware section of society. (There was a strict division between the left and right-wing Ukrainians reflecting mainly adherence to or against Communism and the Soviet system in the U.S.S.R.)

World War I ended in victory for the Allies but with demobilization came unemployment and inflation. Left on their own, without any government assistance whatsoever, the unemployed veterans turned their resentment against those who remained at home, working. Again, the 'foreigners' were blamed.

The Ukrainians, through their left-wing organizations, greeted with enthusiasm the appearance of the revolution in Russia in 1917. Meetings were held, greetings sent and much space devoted in the press to these momentous events. The government responded with banning the clubs, the radical papers were raided, documents seized, active members and leaders arrested, interned and those subject to deportation were deported, (*The Ukrainians in Winnipeg's First Century* by Peter Krawchuk.)

However, no amount of persecution of the radical workers could stay the advance of the economic depression that was engulfing one province after the other. Pushed by poverty, unemployment and the indifference of the powers that be, the workers of Winnipeg went on a general strike in May 1919.

Ukrainians, Poles, Anglos, Scots and Norwegians all struck. Factories were closed, streetcars stopped, theatres darkened, no newspapers appeared and the police and veterans were sympathetic. Encouragement rolled in from the rest of the country. The Provincial and Federal Governments were alarmed. Was this the beginning of revolution here in Canada?

Immediate counter-action was initiated.

The Committee of 1,000 was formed which, reported the Rev. A.E. Smith, "recruited and drilled special constables in schoolyards and barracks. The commanding officer declared that he wanted men who were prepared to shoot to kill...." (see Tim Buck, *A Conscience for Canada*).

This Committee set about to convince everyone that this was a bolshevik revolution. The practice of pitting the native against the foreign-born workers reached its height in a call in the *Winnipeg Free Press* headlined:

The Wretched of the Earth and—Me

UNDESIRABLE CITIZENS IN OUR MIDST

How much longer is the alien to run amuck, to insult our flag, take it by force from Canadian born citizens on the streets, continue this threatening attitude to law and order....(Committee of 1,000)
Winnipeg Free Press,

The strike rolled on to bloody confrontation, to bringing in the North-West Mounted Police, to the reading of the Riot Act, to two killed and 30 wounded during a violent demonstration, to the passing of the Amendment to the Immigration Act (Section 41) providing deportation of 'undesirables' and, finally, the federal government under Sir Robert Borden passed Section 98 of the Criminal Code, which was used for 16 years to shackle and cripple the radical movement. It was finally repealed in 1935.

The General Strike was defeated, its leaders charged not only with leading the strike but, to their total disbelief, with conspiracy to establish Soviet Rule. They were convicted and sent to prison.

No prosperity followed the General Strike. Jobs, however, were still available, although wage cuts, a phenomenon of the late '20s and early '30s, were widespread. The Depression, nevertheless, gained momentum during that decade and by 1932 there were already more than 30,000 receiving relief of some sort in Winnipeg.

How many were penniless and not eligible for relief, including the single unemployed and the newly-created sizeable class of drifters. I was soon to find out when I arrived in Winnipeg in the fall of 1932.

On second glance, Winnipeg was not so alluring. It appeared to me as a conglomeration of impoverished-looking residential areas, shabby shops and shabbier people ambling along. Undoubtedly, the milieu in which I functioned gave me this unhappy impression. I put it all down to the fact that this was a frontier town which cannot be too elegant and this was not a prosperous era. Still, it was depressing and remained so throughout my stay.

The best Charlie could greet me with was "Well, this is Winnipeg." and "You'll like the Harrisons." He had rented a furnished room in the house of a friendly and warm-hearted Ukrainian-Canadian family and that room became our home in Winnipeg.

The next day I was taken to a former church, now the headquarters of the Communist Party and of the Unemployed Association.

That church and the Unemployed Association immediately became my field of activity and I plunged right in, reporting there every morning as though I was punching a clock, or getting paid for it.

The church consisted of a large hall, a stage, some areas behind the wings and, in what had probably been the vestry, our office. I bustled around all day, the only girl amongst about 300 men milling about, all members of the association.

I had a fleeting thought sometimes of what my mother would think of my mixing with these 'rough' men, but most of the time I was concerned with what was happening to them and what should be done about it.

They started arriving about 9 o'clock in the morning and disappeared about 4. I met with small groups, got to know individuals and selected some, Arnold Smith amongst them, who might be trained as activists. We found unemployed journalists, issued four-page newspapers, had them printed and distributed.

The unemployed in Winnipeg were well-organized. They arranged mass meetings, sent delegations to City Council and the Parliament Buildings and lobbied for relief, for shelter.

I did not see anything unusual about being the only female there; in fact, I was quite oblivious of the fact and in my zeal had unconsciously overthrown all sex differentiation. I was quite surprised when Arnold set himself up as my protector, making sure there was no swearing and gallantly tried to introduce some gentility when I was around. "Watch your language," he'd yell. I objected.

"I don't want a *cordon sanitaire* around me. I just want to be treated like a comrade, that's all."

"Well, you're so innocent, for a married woman, I mean."

"I don't know what you are talking about," I flung back at him, annoyed and embarrassed. It was the only 'pass'—if it was a 'pass'—anyone ever made at me while I was working with the unemployed. An overly zealous and compulsive mien was my defence against being approached on any level except the organizational.

The men around the hall were of all ages and of various ethnic origins. Some were British immigrants who came to Canada to work on farms. Others were Ukrainians, Finns or Scandinavians who had been employed in lumber camps or even in the mines.

The Wretched of the Earth and—Me

Relief, which had been $1 a year earlier, was cut off after a while and followed heartbreakingly later by a pitiful handout for which only citizens who could prove legally that they were not transients and had resided in Winnipeg for one year were eligible.

The single unemployed were left out of these benefits. They rallied to their associations and sooner or later came to the 'church.'

Life at the church did not include food or shelter, only organization.

"Where," I asked Arnold, "does everybody go after 4 o'clock?"

"To the jungles, Minnie, to the jungles of the Red River."

Where they sought shelter, it seems, depended on the time of the year. Some prowled the railroad yards and sneaked into empty boxcars for the night. On the banks of the Red River there was shelter of some sort, greater freedom and one could make bon-fires.

Others went to the immigration sheds where the City allowed a limited number to take shelter for a night. At 7 a.m. they were given a crust of bread and ejected from the building, not to be allowed in again until 4 p.m.

Even on the banks of the Red River or in the railroad boxcars they were not allowed to rest in peace. Frequently raided by local police, often while they were asleep, many would be manacled and roughly hauled off to jail. Here they were given shelter of the 30-to-60 days sort, which was not bad except that frequently, many foreign-born were loaded unto trains and delivered to port cities for deportation to whatever country they came from and would have them.

Every day there were members of the association missing who had been seized overnight, arrested or deported or both.

Although the atmosphere was sad and dreary, I was busy night and day. Indeed, I, too, in actuality had no home except the small furnished room at the Harrisons' where there was not even an electric plate on which to make a cup of tea.

Every day we left for the 'hall' early. There were leaflets to be drawn up, organizations contacted for help, clerical work to be done for the Party office, plans made for future activities.

I also had party work to do, participating in current campaigns. We were collecting 100,000 signatures petitioning the federal government for a bill enacting unemployment insurance. I went out frequently, collecting signatures.

The sunshine is deceiving. It is brutally cold, a freezing February afternoon. I am canvassing working-class neighborhoods with a petition. There are only eight lines on the sheet—if I hurry up and get this filled maybe I can go home. (Home? Where is that?) True, I have other sheets. I ring the doorbell. After quite a pause, a lady comes... My God, she is baking! A nostalgic pain stabs... (My mother's hearth on Shabbat eve. Coffee cake and tea by the stove, a job and a weekly pay....) She signs the petition and asks me, somewhat doubtfully, whether I would like to stay for a cup of tea. I refuse and take flight. One must keep away from these middle-class homes where they engage in bourgeois occupations such as baking on Winnipeg's cold, wintry days. It is enough to de-stabilize one's devotion to the task on hand.

I drowned my doubts and feelings of exile in work. "You're a great help to us" said Danny Holmes, the District Party Secretary. "We didn't expect such ability." That was enough for me. I redoubled my efforts, I ran around, intense, devoted, self-important. My good looks, my youth, my small size probably saved me from being considered insufferable. When accused by a member of the Young Communist League of being somewhat of a martinet, I did not necessarily take it as an insult.

After all, the unemployed always said "Ask skinny Minnie over there," when anything needed doing and they didn't mind my being a martinet.

There wasn't much money for food and who could eat with all those hungry souls around all the time? However, at noon we slipped out to Ma's, a nearby restaurant where for 25 cents a very good thick meat stew was served with all the white bread a customer could eat.

There was no time for social activities but in the evenings there were meetings.

These came in all sizes and purposes—to raise money, to direct work in various areas and assign cadres; City committees, District committees, all issuing directives in all directions. As well there were group meetings of the Young Communist League that I attended twice a week, and mass meetings of the unemployed on Market Street, where Charlie was often the principal speaker.

Charlie worked very hard as DO (District Organizer). His daily life consisted of continual Party activity and there was little to provide an uplift from the morass of misery in which we all operated. The pressure of work built up continually as the Depression worsened. Mail poured in daily from all over Manitoba asking for help in dealing with situations where farmers were being dispossessed. Letters in a never-ending stream

The Wretched of the Earth and—Me

poured in from the 'centre' (Toronto), with instructions, suggestions, requests, demands.

I would often find him, bent over the typewriter, working rapidly with two fingers, answering his mail.

This letter was addressed to Sam Carr:

```
Dear Sam:

All kinds of opportunities exist for organizing
units of the Farmers Unity League and the Party.
But, lacking enough developed forces we find it
impossible to put organizers on the road.... To
mobilize properly the forces of revolt on the farm
would require a small army.
I'm sorry, Sam, I'm much too occupied to write
anything original for the paper this month....
During the last few days I've hardly had time to
breath... We had a jobless demonstration last
Thursday. Four thousand marched through mud and
slush  for a mile to the city woodyard. Police
attacked at the finish. Three arrested and some
broken heads...."
```

There was too much work and no amusement or recreation. At any rate, Charlie's amusements were not mine. After addressing mass meetings in Market Square, he and a few others would dash over to a local bootlegger (prohibition was on) and sit by the hour, drinking. I did not drink. I was out of my element and I did not approve of this sort of recreation and the money spent on it.

The misery of the evening was lessened for me by Danny Holmes. Two-and-a-half drinks and the district secretary of the Party would start singing. Glass in hand, his blue eyes closed with emotion, he would relate to us, in Polish song, tales of unrequited love, of pretty girls who had been wronged and of young widows whose husbands would return from battle no more.

The next day it was back to the hall and the never-ending problems of the unemployed.

Not everyone was jobless at this time, although it seemed so to us. Some worked but it was for a pittance. A Youth Conference of the

Workers Unity League (October 19, 1930, Second Session) had well-illustrated the level of these starvation wages:

Jack Hudson had delivered the following report on local industry:

> Dominion Bronze: About 11 young boys employed... wages eighteen and a half cents per hour.
>
> Dominion Bridge and Iron Works: Very young workers taken on. Some work for fifteen cents an hour...
>
> Quality Bed: Working conditions very bad... Brass dust gets into lungs... Minimum wage $12 a week....
>
> Winnipeg Slipper: Sixty pair of shoes must be finished in one hour... A wage of $8 per week is received for this work.
>
> —Ontario Archives, loc - 1820

The organizer, Jack Hudson, concluded his report by urging formation of trade unions for these young exploiteds. However, the only definite result of this continual agitation was reported in *The Worker* in the issue of June 20, 1931. Under the photograph of a pleasant and good-looking young man was the caption:

WRITE TO JACK HUDSON IN WINNIPEG JAIL.

He served one year.

Finally the winter was over and summer came but the unemployed were always with us. In June, the Minister of Labor, Gideon Robertson, arrived in Winnipeg on a "fact-finding tour about unemployment."

Charlie correctly but crudely characterized this as fakery and organized a demonstration outside the minister's quarters. Thousands came and stood silently in front of his hotel, living statistics for his "fact finding."

Unfortunately, it was thought necessary to bring in the police to protect the minister and in attempting to break up the crowd a fight ensued which lasted four hours and which featured barricades and the bringing out of machine guns by the authorities. Demonstrators as well as police were injured and sentences of hard labor in Stoney Mountain Penitentiary were handed out to the unemployed.

It was a busy summer. In July the city closed the only free clinic in

The Wretched of the Earth and—Me

Winnipeg General Hospital and the ensuing protest meeting was again attacked by the police, with tear-gas this time. A further demonstration brought out 20,000 but the clinic stayed closed. (This was not a large crowd to attend a demonstration considering that the unemployed in Canada in 1933 numbered 1.2 million.

In all of these struggles the unemployed were greatly aided by the Communist aldermen in the City Council, William Kolisnyk, Jacob Penner, and others.

It was about this time that Charlie and I noticed that we were being followed continually by a tall, thin young man with a ruddy face.

"It could be a pal of our friend Esselwein," Charlie said, referring to Sergeant Leopold of the R.C.M.P., who had infiltrated the Party in Toronto as Jack Esselwein.

"Well, whoever he is, he's not very effective at shadowing us. He's supposed to follow, not jostle us, for Heaven's sake. He's anything but invisible!"

A few days later, on returning from the hall, an excited Mrs. Harrison met me at the door.

"Minnie, there was a man here. He said he was from the police. He went through your lingerie and things. When he came down he said, 'Oh, so Charlie's wife has arrived...'"

"Just arrived? One of them has been bumping into me for months." I rushed upstairs. Whoever he was, he did not have much to examine. The drawers of the single dresser we had were taken out and everything scattered on the bed and on the floor.

I was horrified but actually instead of being furious at having been 'raided' I was mortified because of scarcity and shabby state of what Mrs. Harrison had politely called my lingerie.

And I was frightened!

"What," I asked Charlie, "is to prevent the R.C.M.P. from nabbing me and sending me off to Roumania like they do to the other foreign-born they pick up on the banks of the Red River?"

I did not much want to be deported back to little Falticeni. Bringing the matter up at a district party meeting for consultation, it was agreed that Section 41 of the Amended Immigration Act did indeed hang darkly over my head. There was a solution, although a desperate one. I could become a Canadian citizen by the simple act of marrying a British citizen and Charlie, born in Manchester, was not unwilling.

Thinking of those long unending sessions at the bootlegger's and my dreary life in Winnipeg I was not too happy about it, but it was the easiest way out.

In the chambers of Judge Lewis St. George Stubbs, with the judge's secretary as witness, we were married and went off gaily to Child's Restaurant for a gala $1 dinner special with a few friends.

"Where is Danny Holmes?" I demanded. "Danny has to be here."

"I didn't want to tell you earlier," said Charlie. "He was picked up at his house last night. They are holding him for deportation."

Under the very Section 41 that I was escaping Danny was held and eventually deported to Poland. A mystified and broken-hearted wife, Marion, and a little daughter were left behind, fatherless and penniless. They were lucky! They had been born in Canada, so they could stay.

The Communist Eight, 1931

Deeply Underground

In August 1931, 'The Communist Eight,' all leaders of the Party, were sentenced to a total of 37 years in Kingston Penitentiary.

Raids by provincial and RCMP on homes and party offices garnered eight leading party personnel—Tim Buck, John Boychuk, Malcolm Bruce, Sam Carr, Tom Hill, Tom McEwen (he gave himself up when he found out he was wanted), Matthew Popowich, Tom Cacic and Mike Gilmore. Charges against Mike Gilmore were dropped, since he was not a member of the Party but of the Young Communist League, which was not mentioned in the indictment. Tons of books were seized, photographs, documents, manuscripts, newspapers and pamphlets. These were subsequently produced as evidence of seditious conspiracy—under Section 98 of the Criminal Code. Proudly produced also, in full red uniform of the Mounties, was Sergeant Leopold, better known to the Party in Toronto as Comrade Jack Esselwein, originally of Austro-Hungary, a more-or-less successful plant of the RCMP. The eight were convicted and sentenced to terms of five years in Kingston Penitentiary. Tom Cacic received two years only but was deported at the end of his sentence.

To avoid having our complete apparatus destroyed by continual raids and the imprisonment of functionaries, we went 'underground.' That, in some cases did not mean more than the stashing away of a duplicating machine in a 'safe house.'

We were great believers in the power and efficacy of the Gestetner copier. With it, every little committee was a success, was securely established as a genuine, functioning organization. The streets having been taken away from us, the leaders jailed, this machine was our approach to the masses. It had to be safely housed and cared for.

Our stipulations for a 'safe' house were not very stringent. The home of any non-Party member was good enough, provided there was an attic room or a good dry cellar where one could spend an hour or two at the machine, communicating with the masses.

Deeply Underground

After I left the Party, even I was asked to play hostess to a Gestetner —much to my bewilderment. I was now a 'safe sympathizer.' Was this a regression or a promotion?

Or we went in for a little disguise by donning dark glasses and, if a male, growing a moustache. One moved around only after dark and after a while, only in the daytime as we banked on the police counting on us to circulate only after sunset.

At first Charlie moved the editorial work of *The Worker* to our third-floor flat on Brunswick Avenue. A courier called Mike, a very young fellow, would come from some place every morning with copy for the paper. To my shame I had to wake Charlie up every time, as he was not an early riser, and the manuscripts had to be placed in his hands only.

The copy was then edited and sent out to the secret print shop for setting, make-up and finally, for printing. Eventually an office was found for this editorial work in a small room next to Mrs. Linzons's kitchen somewhere around Spadina Avenue, in the Annex.

One of the rules for 'underground' life was to move frequently and for a while we found ourselves in a rather grand furnished apartment on the north side of Gerrard Street between Church and Yonge Streets. At that time, the only people who could afford such furnished luxury in that district were prostitutes, but Charlie always regarded prostitutes as being part of the working class.

He investigated the area and the building and pronounced it suitable. We shared these quarters with Anne and Stewart Smith. (A few years later Stewart Smith was to become one of the most popular controllers of the City of Toronto.) I enjoyed the spaciousness of one bedroom for each couple and the living room, dining and kitchen as common areas.

However, we did not enjoy the apartment for long.

Returning from the Young Comrade office on Grenville Street one day —on foot, of course—I found the apartment vacant, our clothes and materials all gone and nothing left but dirty dishes in the sink and a smell of burning paper. When I came out of the building I saw Anne casually strolling by across the road, looking for me, I hoped.

"Where is our stuff? Where is Charlie?" In order of importance

"The boys (Anne always called them 'the boys,' much to my annoyance but I didn't know what to call them either) saw some men in the halls who looked like 'dicks,' so they burnt the critical materials, packed up and left."

The Wretched of the Earth and—Me

"This exercise," I said to myself, "is all due to Stewart's eagerness to put into effect the burning of documents part, which he mixed up with what embassies do. Probably something they told them about at the Lenin Institute. Only we are not an embassy...."

"They are not after us," I informed Anne. "I met the janitor in the hall and he told me the dicks raided some prostitutes on another floor. They weren't even near us." I was very upset at losing our superior quarters.

"Stewart said they looked like dicks, they were dicks and we could not take any chances."

"Doesn't Stewart know the difference between the Vice Squad and the Red Squad?" I persisted, but weakly now, remembering Charlie's rousting return after midnight earlier in the week.

Accompanied by Bill Rigby, visiting editor of a fishermen's weekly newspaper on the West Coast, he returned late at night, waking us up and probably the neighbours as well, with bad renditions of *Molly Malone* and a ribald version of *Oh Susannah*. Charlie claimed the next day that they had broken street lights as well and that he was following a holy tradition.

"Karl Marx always broke street lamps when he was out of a night in London, unwinding after a hard day of writing *Das Kapital* in the British Museum," he explained. I think Charlie felt that breaking street lamps would somehow put him in touch with Karl Marx, at least place him in the category of people who unwind that way.

Charlie could always find amazing precedents for his predilection for alcoholic binges, starting of with Omar Khayam and ending with Baudelaire. He claimed that Baudelaire advocated:

> *Always be drunken;*
> *Be drunken with women;*
> *Be drunken with song;*
> *Be drunken with love;*
> *But always be drunken.*

Had Charlie blown our cover?

I conceded that we had to leave—indeed, had already left—these contaminated premises and joined Anne in planning our next move.

We parted company at this point, Stewart and Anne going underground on Davenport Road, just west of Bathurst Street. And I, spoilt by living

Deeply Underground

in a suite instead of a single room, dipped into my 'accident' fund, which I was guarding for when I was "going to leave Charlie" (I was always planning to leave Charlie; in the fall I would say "in the spring" and in the spring I would say "in the fall") and rented a furnished flat. It was above a store on Bloor Street West just across Robert and was luxurious by the standard of the '30s, giving rise to supposedly humorous remarks about 'Moscow Gold' on the part of one or two co-workers who were allowed to visit us.

I never did have all the rules of underground life explained to me thoroughly. First of all, we changed our names. For a while we ran riot on that, unofficially that is, and had fun with pseudonyms. The Duke, the Spanish Hen, the Pea Fowl, the Fop, were rampant. One communicated with others as little as possible, used the telephone sparingly, spoke in monosyllables and some devised impossible-to-follow codes.

Disguise was important but didn't extend to women, much to my sorrow. Having contact with as few people as possible was important and, if feasible, we left town.

Anne and Stewart Smith got to live in a summer resort for a while and others scattered to various cities, New York particularly. There, they took to writing books and pamphlets.

I questioned Charlie severely about those sent underground to the U.S.A. "What kind of directives can they give from New York?" I complained. I could understand them coming from Kingston Penitentiary, but New York?

"Lenin did, from Switzerland and darn well, too. Witness the Russian Revolution."

I mulled this over very carefully and for some time I half expected the Canadian revolution, if it came at all, to come from New York.

Some confused the period of living underground with power failures and blackouts and understood this to be a proper time to have children and attend to their political nurturing. Hence, at the time of the Spanish Civil War, male children were appropriately named Norman (viz. Dr. Bethune) and girls Dolores (viz. Ibaruri), thus giving them a good start in life.

Nonetheless, husbands were separated from wives, children were reared without fathers, the R.C.M.P. followed the women to lead them to their mates even as far as New York and there was a great deal of pain and sorrow.

On the Banks of the French River

My friend Taimi Davis, née Pitkanen, was pregnant, which was a disaster on many levels. Their little flat on Peter Street south of Queen Street was always clean, as only Finns understand clean, and on Sundays there was often a roast of beef with Yorkshire pudding (for Jim, the Anglo-Saxon husband) to which I cadged all the invitations I could. However, the scantiness of the furniture and furnishings bespoke of the poverty in which party organizers lived. A baby would demand food, diapers, medicine, a carriage, a cot, clothes and heaven knows what else. Where was it all to come from?

Always the planner, I cast about in my mind for a solution. A partial solution? What about a rummage sale? (But we could not raise money for private ends.)

I lived in a flat, bed-sitting-room and kitchen, further north, in the comparatively well-to-do district of Henry Street. I had contact with comrades who were regarded as affluent, some working, others who owned small shops or had connections with business people.

"I know what," I said. "A shower! A baby shower!"

My landlady consented to the use of her living room downstairs (she was a 'sympathizer') and I rushed to use her telephone. I was good at soliciting by phone.

On the agreed-upon evening when Jim and Taimi arrived in answer to my mysterious invitation, they were ecstatic. On the floor was a clothes hamper overflowing with baby things and milling around were many friends amidst a reassuring odor of brewing coffee.

"Look, Jim" said Taimi, "baby oil, diapers, Pablum, little dresses and bottles, blankets and even some money." Some told of a doctor who would deliver the baby free of charge and someone else knew a nurse.

All were most anxious to help and share, for to share was to survive.

Whatever would have become of us were it not be for those saints in the movement who had more than others and who lived by the dictum "live simply that others may simply live."

Such was Helen Burpee and the other members of the Sutcliffe family. Coming as she did of affluent parents—her grandfather had actually been Whip in the Conservative Party in Ontario at one time, in addition to which she and her husband were well-established accountants. She could have led a comfortable middle-class life. Instead, she, and all her family, pared it down by sharing not only earnings but lifestyles.

The tired and the poor among the activists were often invited to the family 'camp' on the French River. I was to find out eventually that this was not really a 'camp' but a fine summer home, supplemented by cabin-sized sleeping porches built on the property.

Such an invitation provided my first real holiday in years.

"Come after the black-fly-season is over," said Helen. "Let's say, August."

I left the travel arrangements to her.

Cars being rare objects, we travelled by train to Pickerel Station and then—much to my astonishment—by canoe to the 'camp,' which was on a spit of land almost entirely surrounded by water. Everything was new to me, especially canoeing.

Apparently the Sutcliffes were all adept at this, as was shown by photographs on the camp mantelpiece depicting various members of the family in or near canoes, portaging canoes, struggling in choppy water in canoes, or paddling canoes furiously surrounded by madly churning angry waves.

That this was not something that happened long ago, but an everyday activity I found out a few days later on a planned trip to Ricollet Falls. With the immense, ominous gray cliffs of the 'French' towering over us on both sides, above the boiling waters, Mrs. Sutcliffe and Helen 'ran the rapids' on their knees on little flat cushions while I hunkered down, kneeling for dear life astern, frightened to death but convinced that this is the right stance for inhabiting a canoe.

Once landed, we rested above the falls, then I bravely threw in a fishing line. So plentiful were the pickerel that I caught one immediately, which Mrs. Sutcliffe fried in butter right there and then. On the return journey I witnessed an Indian going upriver being helped to portage both canoe and supplies over Ricollet Falls by a man from the French River Trading and Outfitting Co. "Where is he going?" I asked. To me this was already the end of the world.

"Georgian Bay, Georgian Bay," was the shouted reply. Was that

The Wretched of the Earth and—Me

possible? To go up river and get to Georgian Bay? How wonderful Canada is.

I was hooked on fishing and the next day I caught a rock bass from among many lazily swimming off the back porch. "At this time of the year, Minnie," said Mrs. Sutcliffe gently rejecting my offer, "The rock bass are inclined to be wormy. Why don't you take a line and go out and catch yourself a pickerel?"

I grabbed a fishing rod and paddled over to a nearby platform left on the river by an abandoned saw mill. I dropped the line among floating logs and it was immediately snapped up by a wildly voracious, fighting pickerel. After a struggle I was able to land it on the platform, only to have it rudely break the line and make its getaway with the artificial bait, spoons and all.

I ran back complaining.

"You need a landing net," said Helen, "And you'd better get some minnows for bait."

Some minnows were collected in a pail and the next day I caught a fish but the minnows had to be impaled on the hook, which I did with my head averted. For a while, my enthusiasm for catching fish fought with the necessity of being unspeakably cruel to minnows.

Then came a day when, at twilight, I went out with a line and Helen followed with the landing net and we both veered away from the dock and watched the sunset instead. Said Helen: "I guess we have enough fish." And we went indoors and ate divided chocolates.

Mrs. Sutcliffe's knowledge of sharing extended to many levels. The large Secord candies I brought in the half-pound box were divided into two, maybe three sections, which made for variety, equality and cozy comradeship.

I learned much from the Sutcliffes but their precepts could not always be followed.

Sometimes financial problems had to be solved in a drastic way, as on the occasion when, despite my disapproval, Charlie packed our scanty belongings in a suitcase and we made our way out quickly after midnight. We owed two weeks rent for a room on Spadina Avenue to a poor Finnish landlady and so we 'skipped.' Mrs. Sutcliffe and Helen would not have approved of that rotten little escapade.

Food and rent were difficult enough to come by but illnesses and babies were a catastrophe. Such an impending catastrophe led Sarah

Goldstick to gather up some money at a Marxist study group, conducted by Charlie, which bought the wicker baby carriage (and an astounding $25 in cash) presented to me when my son was born.

Later in the Depression, living on relief at 750 Spadina Avenue, the allowance of $2.25 a week the city provided would not have sustained two adults and a baby were it not for the assistance, again, of Helen Burpee. Employed as an accountant by various left-wing businesses, she came around every week bringing butter, Pablum, oranges and tobacco for the 'makings' for Charlie from the Co-op grocery stores that could not always pay her in cash.

Party organizers were expected to be self-reliant and practically self-supporting. Like the armies of old, when on organizational tours, we were supposed to live off the land as far as food was concerned, although money for travelling was advanced by whatever committee set up the trip. For Instance:

```
St. Catharines. Ont.
24th.July, 1931
Dear Comrade:
Please find enclosed tickets for Toronto-Queenston
boat for your transportation here July 27th.
Bring pamphlets BENNETT'S STARVING BUDGET.


(signed) J.Faulkner
```

(Ontario Archives 5B 0801)

Goat Mountain

Sent on a tour of the West to organize or resuscitate Young Pioneer groups (the fare of $67.50 return by rail was a great inducement to organization), the National Executive Committee of the Young Communist League made me an allowance for 'coffee and' but that was all. I didn't seem to be too worried. I remembered my mother's "*Got vilt helfen*" on the way from Roumania.

On the train going west I met Edward Yardas, organizer for the Croat Organization, who most graciously shared a roast chicken with me from the lunch someone had packed for him. Day two, I dipped into my 'coffee and' fund and bought some apples and cookies, sharing them, as I was taught, with a young woman who apparently wasn't eating much either. To my disgust, she got up and, walking a few seats forward, gave my precious apples to two nuns seated there. Sharing had its problems!

In the towns where I stopped the comrades always saw to it that I was fed, difficult as that must have been for them. (I remember the dinners but not much of the mass meetings I addressed). In Moose Jaw I was invited to share 'eats' with a young married couple who subsisted on a side of beef sent to them by their parents on the family farm. This beef was pickled in brine and every day they cut off a portion, which, fried or roasted, made wonderful meals.

In Blairemore, Alta., which boasted of a street named Tim Buck Boulevard, I was invited to the home of an Italian miner. The lady of the house brought to the table a magnificent platter, heaped impossibly high with spaghetti. Covered by the spaghetti was a whole chicken, an unforgettable sight.

It was in Blairemore, as well, that a very intuitive friend arranged a hike into the mountains for me, providing an experience the memory of which has never faded.

"You are going up Goat Mountain with my sister Sarah," said Isobel Murphy, my hostess.

Goat Mountain

At eight in the morning and the time was early April, we started out on a footpath winding itself through bush and evergreens and going higher, ever higher. It was not until about 2 o'clock in the afternoon that the vegetation began to disappear and bare rock became visible but not predominant.

It was colder now, the odd snowflake drifted down and when we reached the summit, Sarah somehow managed to create a fire and from a backpack produced another miracle—a steak to fry and a pan to fry it in. We rested. The gray and green and even mauve of rocks and trees, the sharp tang of chill in the air, the thick odor of pine needles and the never broken silence enveloped us in an intoxicating mist.

"Let's stay here forever and ever," I suggested—like a new kind of Lotus-eater weary of striving—but Sarah had other ideas and insisted we commence the descent without delay. Soon, the feelings of regret disappeared and we giggled and sang all the way down, our cares washing away the magic of Goat Mountain.

When I arrived in Vancouver the local Pioneer leader and my hostess, Annie Rossman (eventually to become a lifelong friend), grabbed all my clothes and rushed them off to the cleaners. Having one's clothes cleaned professionally was a great luxury in the Depression. Usually we sponged-cleaned such items that could not be laundered, by simply using an iron and a damp press cloth, which was what we did *en-route*.

In B.C. there was bread and roses, too, for me. Not only were people dining and breakfasting me but I was taken to English Bay, where the daffodils were already in bloom. Girls were wearing white shoes and people were going hatless. Truly, this was the loveliest part of the country, if only it were not the province where the youth of the land was toiling for 25 cents a day in work camps hidden in the mountains.

Nor were things better for the unemployed in the cities. Heads of families were desperate. One wrote to *The Worker*:

```
Mr. I. Griffiths
2540 Burns St.
Vancouver BC
Dear Editor:
I am a reader of your paper and a member of the
Communist Party of Vancouver. I would like you to
publish this little note.
```

The Wretched of the Earth and—Me

I am a married man with a wife & children age 9-6-2-9 months. I get 4 dollars & 25 cents of food for a week. I have to go without myself to give the children the food. I have been on relief 7 months I only got 1 load of wood and now I need it to make food they will not give it to me they told me to go and pick my wood where I would like to know the only place I could pick wood from is the C.N.R. tracks I went there to get some but the C.N.R. flat feet came after me and made me put it down. I went to see (Our famous Col. Cooper) but I only got as far as ... Kemp ... he said ... you had better see Mr. Minchen the snake.... He told me he will send the investigator out but I am still waiting.
I am about 3 lbs., of meat for six and 2 lbs of that is bone. I asked the boutcher for a little more meat and he said what the hell do you want for nothing....
Dear Sir, I would like you to word this better for print.
I remain yours truly,
Mr. I. Griffiths

(Ont. Archives, 4A 2656)

While the young unemployed men were sent to the workcamps, the plight of the single homeless girls was probably the worst of any section of the unemployed in Vancouver. It was difficult to get relief, they were always told to go into domestic service. Ronald Liversedge writes in *Recollections of the On-to-Ottawa Trek* that "the wage for a domestic servant at that time was ten dollars a month. Girls were actually told by relief officers that with their figure they shouldn't have to seek relief."

"Vancouver was a hectic place; skirmishes took place every day at the relief offices. On the street some individuals, in desperation, would smash in store windows to obtain food and shelter for a while—in jail."

The unemployed organized. Leaders arose. One, Allan Campbell, headed parades, continually addressed unemployed meetings, led deputations demanding relief and reaped the fury of the authorities.

Goat Mountain

Following an open-air meeting, a delegation was sent with the demands of the unemployed to City Council. Five days later Campbell and fellow activist Cunningham were arrested and charged with "inciting to riot." Following further demonstrations, Campbell was arrested again while addressing the workers from the Cenotaph and charged with "unlawful assembly." Although the original charge was "inciting to riot," a few days before the trial another count was added— "uttering seditious words." He was sentenced to one year in prison, and ordered to be deported to England. (Prov. of Ont. Archives 21H 1167).

The concern with hunger, with actually getting enough to eat, motivated most of our actions.

If I thought too much about food during my tour of the West, it was because I was hungry very often or probably just malnourished, as were thousands of others during the aptly named 'Hungry Thirties.' My instinct for self-preservation, or maybe just greed, kept me fed somehow during those lean years. Others were not so lucky!

Jack Little, who was also sent out organizing, died, if not entirely from starvation then because malnutrition had reduced his resistance to nil. He was brought to Toronto and laid out in the living room of Mrs. Arland on St. Mary Street.

I recalled his china-blue eyes and seeing him lying there, so blond, so young and so very emaciated, I wept.

"Who killed you, Jack Little, who really killed you?" As a member of the National Executive Committee of the Young Communist League, I had voted to his being sent out as organizer. Was I guilty too?

Would his chance of survival have been better had he been riding the rails up and down the country like everyone else—looking through a factory window watching people work ("How I envied them," he had recounted to me) or perhaps, like Irving Salson of Toronto, he would have 'just' lost a leg riding the rods and have survived to employment and better times.

A few met other dangers besides starvation. One of our girl organizers who was sent out on a tour suffered a romantic encounter. She came back pregnant. However, there wasn't much of that. The great menace for party activity, as for millions of Canadians, was hunger.

There were a few successes — surprisingly, more than a few.

Dave White was given $2 and a pair of second-hand trousers and encouraged to ride the rods or hitch-hike to Fort William and Port

The Wretched of the Earth and—Me

David and Clara White, Toronto, 1930

Arthur, the whole area being assigned to him to organize. And he did just that, successfully placing the Young Communist League on its feet and strengthening the trade union movement. He even brought his eighteen-year-old fiancée, Clara, out of Montreal and put her in charge of the Young Pioneers. Unable to find a rabbi, they had to make do with a Lutheran minister, who was not prejudiced at all. He most willingly married them.

The Worker

Hungry or not, we had to carry on the struggle against the Depression and for that, our voice, *The Worker*, had to be maintained.

The Party groups were the backbone of the financial structure. Party personnel could scrounge around to keep alive and working but the party press had to be supported on a cold-cash basis. Nickel and dime contributions and all sorts of money-raising activities by Party members, 'left-wing' organizations and radical supporters kept the party press, particularly *The Worker*, afloat.

When I first joined the movement, we all subscribed to a theoretical journal called the *Canadian Labor Monthly*. It featured articles by world-famous theoreticians such as R. Palm Dutt.

The list of subscribers embraced many who were to become devoted activists for the Party for decades to come. Included was 'J. Esselwein,' alias Sergeant Leopold of the R.C.M.P., who was listed as living in "Allan Gardens Apts. Carlton Street."

The Canadian Labor Monthly

Name	Address	Subscription
M. Davis	188 Palmerston Avenue	6 Months
Shirley Ethlin	104 Grace Street	"
A. Kohn	294 Robert Street	"
H. Munroe	28 Wellington Street East	"
Mrs. F. Custance	211 Milverton Blvd.	"
Vienna Tionenen	54 Wedmere Street	"
W. Bosovich	500 Bathurst Street	"
W. Kent	575 Keele Street	"

The Wretched of the Earth and—Me

Walter Swift	575 Keele Street	6 Months
J. Esselwien	Allan Garden Apts., Carlton Street	"
S. Goodis	277 Grace Street	"
J. Blugerman	277 Grace Street	"
W. Sydney	219 Robert Street	"
A. Alquist	27 Acorn Street	"
Sam Cohen	450 Spadina Avenue	"
Mrs. Shur	433 Montrose Avenue	"
Miss E. Fender	54 Victor Avenue	"
M. Gershman	450 Spadina Avenue	1 Year
H. Guralniek	353 Grace Street	"
Beckie Buhay	353 Grace Street	"
Bert Robinson	19 Elmwood Avenue	"
C. Marriott	235 Major Street	"
A. Vaqara	206 Broadview Avenue	"
A. Reisberg	164 Borden Street	"
Davis Quarter	158 Lippencote Street	"
Fred Peel	83 Lavinia Avenue	"
Jack Valen	820 Pape Avenue	"
R. Shoesmith	1964 Gerrard Street East	"
Thos. Skene	54 Victor Avenue	"
Alice Buck	54 Delaney Crescent	"
P. Halpern	450 Spadina	"
Jack Macdonald	54 Victor Avenue	"
M. Bernstein	175 Lippencott Street	"
G. Ketcheson	158 Beaconsfield	"
M. Mann	125 Sincoe Street	"
Tom Burpee	28 Wellington Street East	"

To ensure the continued existence of the *Canadian Labour Monthly,* and *The Worker* we organized all kinds of dances, socials and cultural affairs and Party Box Lunches. For these, the girls prepared a lunch in a gaily decorated box and the men or boys bid for them, getting to eat the food with the girl who provided it, which I thought was romantic and Victorian, although not exactly overflowing with culture.

The Worker, published weekly at this time, sold for 5 cents a copy and its subscription rate was only $2 a year, $1 for six months. They sent out free sample copies "on request."

Subscriptions, money, dribbled in.

July, 1931

To *The Worker*
94A Church Street

Comrades:
Enclosed you will find one dollar bill.... Please send me *The Worker* for six months.... Wrap good *The Worker* in plain paper before you send it to me and don't spell my name in full.
(signed) W.O.
Box 228,
Kapuskasing, Ont.

(Ont. Archives, 5B 0804)

Kyle, Sask. July 1931

The Worker:
Dear Comrades:
Enclosed $2.00 as yearly sub. for J. Douglas of Matador, Sask.
This subscriber is section boss on the C.P.R.....
(Signed) W. Searle

(Ont. Archives, 56B 0805)

It was not enough.

In the summer of 1930, Jeanne Corbin, an unemployed school teacher, was sent on a national tour to raise money for *The Worker*. Again, money was raised in dribs and drabs but she was very careful to account for every penny and always sent detailed statements to *The Worker* office.

The Wretched of the Earth and—Me

Montreal
May 22, 1930
The Worker
650 Bay Street
Toronto

Dear Comrade:
Enclosed is a complete report from Montreal. The total amount enclosed is $80.86.... I have deducted my fare and expenses and I am sending you a receipt so you can make a cheque for deposit and enter same as 'sale expense.'
Please do not publish the names of those who donated but only the initials....

With Communist Greetings
Jeanne H. Corbin,
The Worker organizer

June 20th. Jeanne
"..I am sending you $20.00 all I have on hand just now as I know you are broke ... seeing that Timmins did not pay expenses....."

July 8th. 1930.
Port Arthur, Ont.
Receipts
   $51.40

Expenditures:
Fare- Sudbury - Port Arthur $20.50
Expenses $10.90
Sent to Worker $20.00

                      $51.40

(Ont. Archives 7B 1768)

The Worker

Thin, intense, small in stature and dark in complexion, fatigued and worn out at all times, Jeanne did not indulge herself even to the extent of an extra cup of coffee. Every cent had to be sent in and she was religiously meticulous and painstaking in her accounting.

```
Montreal, Que. May 22,1930
Financial Statement

    Newsubs............................    19.00
    Renewals                              27.00
    Donations                             39.00
                                          85.00
    Fare and expenses                     18.00
    Amount sent National office.........  67.00
    Worker bundles.                       13.86
    Total amount enclosed                $80.86
```

(Ont. Archives 7B1797)

Money was scarce, nickels and dimes counted, there was little to spare for luxuries such as reading material, even when your heart was with *The Worker*, as outlined by A. Bridenko, a contributor.

```
Kirkland Lake, July 1931
Dear Comrades:
I have a few lines to write about working
conditions in Kirkland Lake.
When I was in Sudbury last winter I heard lots of
people talking about K.L.(Kirkland Lake), the
mines being in full swing.... I left Sudbury and
was in pretty near every city in Eastern Ontario.
At last I came to K.L. with hope, to get a job in
the mines. When I came here I found that there
were around a thousand men without work.
Every day I see hundreds of men standing at the
main gates. Some days I see a few women with
baby's in their arms, begging the bosses to give a
job to their husbands. But the bosses do not pay
```

The Wretched of the Earth and—Me

any attention to them any more. Allways they answer the same thing, nothing doing today.... At night there are fires burning around the town. These are the men who are sleeping in the bush. We had a demonstration here and the next day the "city fathers" gave two days work to a few men to make enough to get out of town.
(Signed) Bridenko

The Worker, subsequently named *The Clarion* and then *The Canadian Tribune*, managed to survive, but not Jeanne Corbin. She died of tuberculosis in Northern Ontario.

(Ont. Archives 4A 2561)

Paid functionaries of the Party, like Jeanne Corbin, like Jack Little, contributed everything they had to the movement. Some unwittingly threw in their wives and children.

Death in Karelia

Aate Pikanen and his father, c. 1930

Like an evil maelstrom, the Depression had a way of thrusting people into many an impossible, life-threatening vortex and then spewing them out again. Some didn't survive.

"Minnie, I'm afraid my brother is dead," said my friend Taimi over the telephone one day, her usual bubbling enthusiasm hushed by sorrow.

"Some people just came back from Finland, around Lake Ladoga, and talked about it." I knew her brother had been away for some years and remembered him, Aate Pitkanen, as a tall, blond young man, very polite, very restrained, "riding the rods" to Toronto to visit his married sister and staying on for a while.

The Wretched of the Earth and—Me

Taimi understood. "The poor kid. What is there to do in Port Arthur for a single young guy out of a job? He may as well hang around here for a bit."

And then, early in 1931, in the depths of the Depression, an article appeared in a Toronto newspaper that changed the course of his life. This article, subsequently reprinted in *The Worker* and other newspapers, stated that there was a shortage of labour in the Soviet Union.

The word spread from mouth to mouth; from Vernon, B.C., to Edmonton, Alberta., from Winnipeg to Hamilton to Niagara Falls to Kirkland Lake to Moose Jaw and to Rouyn, Quebec. *The Worker* was inundated with inquiries and those in the know wrote personally to Tim Buck. Precious skilled labour, rejected and unwanted in Canada, cried out its wares.

At the bottom of a letter from Rouyn, Que., someone in *The Worker* office had pencilled in:

```
No agents in Canada. May write to Amtorg,
261 - 5th. Ave. New York
```

This was the trade mission which the Soviet Union maintained in New York. It is doubtful if many, or any, of the skilled workers who wrote to Tim Buck or *The Worker* found their way to the Soviet Union but an organized group of skilled Finnish woodsmen, some being members of the Lumberworkers' Union, The Finnish Organization of Canada and even of the Communist Party, made the necessary arrangements and departed for Finland.

They were more or less welcomed in Soviet Karelia (the Karelians are one of the three basic ethnological stocks making up Finland), where most of them were born. They were skilled labourers, ready to leave their homes in Canada, where their ability and craft was not wanted, and prepared to give the benefit of their know-how to those that needed it, the Soviet workers. It was good to be employed, to have one's skill used.

The primary plan was to work for two years, aiding the Karelian lumber industry and return to North America at the end of that period. They left in small groups, spread out over a period of two years. There might have been a minimum of 300 men from Canada, more from the United States. Those who went were single men and those who were married left their families in North America.

Death in Karelia

They took their tools with them. The Soviet Government wanted not only the skill of the men but also their tools and requested that they demonstrate to, and train Soviet workers in, 'American' lumbering technology.

There was a sort of understanding that if they didn't take out Soviet citizenship, they would stay for two years.

"What have we got to lose? It'll be good to work for a while."

Aate was a graduate of a technical school in Port Arthur, had studied communications and had worked as a telephone linesman. He certainly would have appreciated some work in his chosen trade and quickly agreed to go.

They landed in Matroosa, the centre of Soviet Karelia's lumbering industry, but because of his specialty Aate went on to Petrozavodsk, north of Lake Ladoga, the capital of Karelia. He was employed as a telephone linesman and later in a vital technical capacity having to do with the set-up of the telephone system of the city. His father returned to the family in Canada after one year but Aate stayed on.

"His letters showed how contented he was," said Taimi. "It was good to have work, to be appreciated, to have scope for his skills." He excelled in sports, particularly skiing, came in second in the All-Union Slalom Competition and became a ski instructor.

He married, adjusted well and was happy for some years.

Then came the year 1937 and the Nazi attack.

After a short breathing spell, afforded by the Nazi-Soviet Pact, the invasion of Soviet Karelia was swift. Petrozavodsk was occupied by the Germans and the right-wing Finns. There was nowhere to flee, but Aate could fight back. He joined the partisans and actively assisted the resistance but not for long.

Short is the lifespan of a guerilla fighter.

Aate and a co-worker, an American Finn who had come to Karelia at the same time and had worked with him on the telephone system, were captured by the Nazi with the assistance of the local Quislings.

The Nazi demanded the layout plans of the telephone exchanges and other technical information. This was refused. They were tortured and still they resisted.

Finally, Aate Pitkanen, the Canadian, and Laatinen, the American, were executed together by the Germans. Aate's wife perished at the same time.

The Wretched of the Earth and—Me

"At least they died fighting the Nazi," said Taimi.

Other 'volunteers' were not so fortunate.

Even before the Second World War broke out, returning Finns brought back strange stories of some of their comrades' disappearances. Stalin's insane doubting mania was at its height. It needed but a whisper and the dreaded raid in the night spelled setting out along a road from which few returned.

After the war, all populations which had been occupied by the Nazi were suspect. It was easy to pin suspicion on these newcomers from capitalist Canada and from the very home of capitalism, the United States of America. Informers were busy.

'American' immigrants were denounced to Beria and to his secret service apparatus, the K.G.B. Beria, it was said, was only too happy to prove his loyalty to Stalin by producing another pool of 'enemies of the state.'

No one knows for sure how many died. North American friends and relatives would suddenly receive no mail. Inquiries among others who had gone to Karelia with them elicited only the reply that they had disappeared one day and no one knows where they were and dared not ask.

Those who remained Canadian citizens did not fare too badly. The lethal hand of the K.G.B. fell on such who, out of loyalty to their Communist ideals, took out Soviet citizenship.

Seeking only to lead a simple, useful workingman's life, rejected and condemned to unemployment and sheer starvation by their heartless and uncaring government, these Canadians became enmeshed in the agony of the times, eked out a pitiful existence and died a ruthless and meaningless death.

"Even though they died in Finland, they were victims of the cruel Canadian Depression," I said, trying to sum it up for Taimi, but there was no consolation in it.

Back in the Mainstream

The hungry '30s were followed by the victorious forties and by the enlightened '50s. We had fought to make the world safe for democracy and new ideas flooded the nation, from open-air cafes on Bloor Street to family allowance. The very Liberal party whose leader, Mackenzie King, had said "Not a red nickel" in relief to the unemployed, now passed legislation for unemployment insurance and the Opposition once led by 'Iron Heel Bennett,' who had vowed "We will not put a premium on idleness or put our people on the dole," now meekly voted assent.

Our strident calls across the forests and prairies of the land crying for relief from hunger and insecurity for so many years in vain, were now joined by other voices, louder still and at this time more influential. The Co-Operative Commonwealth Federation (CCF) came into being and the Liberal Party, responding at last to the need for change, took these now reasonable planks into their platform and added old age and veterans' pensions, and widows' and mothers' allowances.

Even the hitherto outrageous demands initiated by the Young Pioneers for free school lunches and wading pools in the parks became reasonable and possible. A new philosophy advocated purchasing power for the masses to keep industry humming. It was working. Cheques were going out to every family, $6 a month for every child up to the age of 16. There was money for shoes and sweaters and some of it was even put aside by the mothers for the children's education.

The C.I.O. (Committee for Industrial Organization) was replacing the old craft unions and organizing the unorganized, even the textile workers of Hamilton. The demand for consumer goods, interrupted during the war, kept everyone employed.

We had 'prosperity,' a new welcome word. The 'Red Squad' in Toronto went out of existence. The R.C.M.P. slacked in their zeal of chasing known Communists; retaining files on them, however.

There was a moderate amount of rejoicing in the land. But somehow, we in the movement, were not part of this. We were reluctant to admit that things were going well in the Party, we were critical.

The Wretched of the Earth and—Me

It is not enough to have bread. The C.C.F. was 'reformist;' the trade unions were engaged in throwing the left wing out and Winston Churchill was busy shutting the Soviet bloc behind an 'Iron Curtain.'

We withdrew into ourselves more and more, becoming a narrow sect.

Whereas during the '30s we had the pulse of the people, voicing their needs and leading, now we were dragging behind, full of ifs and buts and pulling up our ideological skirts, keeping pure and making sure we were not being besmirched by reformism and co-operation with the bosses.

Ah, but I was enjoying prosperity myself. Will I ever forget the thrill of my first paycheque of $15 and the anticipation of another just like it the following week! With my first pay I frivolously bought a pair of black, patent leather pumps and a small suitcase for weekends at Camp Naivelt.

My mother, a widow again, was free to keep house for my little son and me. My salary seemed adequate for a three-room flat rented at $25 a month on Euclid Avenue and which was happily situated right near the West End *Creche*. And then there was the 'baby bonus' of $6 coming in every month.

An array of consumer goods made its way cautiously into our flat; a bedroom set bought on the installment plan for my son, a 'hollywood divan' for me to sleep on in the living room, bits of linen and clothes.

Back into the main stream, I discovered night-school courses and ran in joy from swimming at Central Tech. to 'Anthropology' at the University of Toronto.

At the office there were seven workmates with whom I made friends. I easily accepted the fact that they were not politically inclined, all but one, and that one was a Conservative with whom I was chummy as well. I kept my political proclivities to myself and organized only a 'Joy and Recreation Club.' A five-cents-a-week contribution by everyone in the office created a fund which bought cake and ice cream on every birthday.

Following my new line of being friendly with everyone, I took these sweets in to the private offices of our two bosses, who thanked us politely, complaining only that they suspected every employee had at least three birthdays a year.

After I left the overall manufacturing to go into cutlery, I met Mr. Morawetz, my former employer, one day on a streetcar and we chatted.

"But those were the best years of my life, I loved being with Carhartts," I admitted.

"Good! At least you have good memories. But tell me. are you still with that, that...Communist Party?"

" Nooo, not quite. But how did you know?" I replied, being suddenly doubtful of my committment.

"Two policemen came during the war, I think they were from the R.C.M.P. They asked if you were behaving yourself."

"So what did you say?"

"I told them you were into demanding ice cream for the masses."

"And what did they say?"

"They were writing it all down and I told them it's o.k., we were safe. They could go away now."

My best friend was Jenny, a Baptist. I had never met a Baptist before and discovered to my amazement that she didn't go to dances, abstained from tea, coffee, movies and alcohol, and was very moral and upright in every way.

In fact, she was very much like a Communist—only more so, she never criticized nor preached. Pretty, petite, she charmed everyone in her path.

After her marriage to another avidly committed Baptist, she would only work part-time but everyone was busy finding jobs for her as, during the war, efficient secretaries were scarce. Our office manager was very insistent on an offer from a garment manufacturer on Spadina Avenue.

"My friends have a very good job for you, Jennie. Just name your salary." Jenny consulted her husband and explained that the income tax on their combined 'take-home pay' would be too high to make it worthwhile for her to be fully employed.

"I'll tell you what," was the next offer, "My friends will pay your salary out of petty cash and you won't have any taxable income at all." Whereupon Jenny reported that her husband had definitely said "No"—it would not be fair to "cheat the government out of income tax."

Spadina Avenue manufacturers, some of whom were busily squirreling away cash in safety deposit boxes to avoid paying 'excess profits tax,' chuckled about that one for weeks.

Back at my weekly meetings of the Communist Party, I was overrunning with zeal again.

"We must go out among the people," I urged. "Look at our activities! What are we doing? Busy taking in each other's washing. Selling one another tickets to dull affairs which no one attends, except ourselves. We must break out."

The Wretched of the Earth and—Me

Week after week I became more concerned that we were a small sect, ingrown, more concerned with matters abroad than what is going on in our own country.

I was disturbed, in addition, about the 'trials' in the Soviet Union and the adulation of Stalin.

I didn't like Joseph Stalin.

I resented having to stand up for the ovations he received at meetings large and small. I, who had refused to stand up for *God Save The King* now had to stand for Stalin. I muttered every time I rose to my feet and grumbled my dissent.

I pictured to myself the trials, the sentencing to infamous work-camps for heretics and all suspected of being heretics. Him, the dictator, with Beria (Secret service-G.P.U. chief) at his side going over lists, sentencing, killing.... It was stupid to accept his pronouncements as the alpha and omega of everything—what kind of an expert could he be on heredity, for instance? What if I didn't stand up, would a committee be appointed immediately to investigate the crime of my seat-edness?

And now *Cosmopolitanism* was a crime. I liked cosmopolitanism, that is what I joined the movement for, for its internationalism, for its belief that all humans, regardless of color or creed, are brothers. Cosmopolitanism, indeed! Was that just an excuse for the hidden anti-semitism of Stalin, Brezhnev and so many others right inside the Communist Party of the Soviet Union? It was because of my whole-hearted adherence to internationalism that I was lukewarm and indifferent to the emergence of the State of Israel.

I wish they would leave us alone, I wish that the Party in Canada would pursue its own aims, in its own way.

But there was no sign of that. Dissent in Canada was also stamped out, although mercifully without Gulags.

Then Khrushchev came along. At the 20th Congress of the Communist Party of the Soviet Union, Stalin and his crimes were condemned, a draft of fresh air came into the dank, stale atmosphere of the Communist Parties, only to have the door closed again under Breznev and the principle of the leading role of the Communist Party of the Soviet Union insisted upon, by means of guns, if necessary, and it seems to have been necessary in Hungary and Czechoslovakia.

"If you are not with us all the way, you are against us," they said.

But I wanted to be friends with people who came with us only half way, people who fought anti-semitism and racism, who were anti-war and not necessarily pro-Soviet, people who signed petitions and did not believe in the revolution.

In fact, I liked the C.C.F. (Co-operative Commonwealth Federation), and had a great deal of respect for its members. They only went half way, sure, but part of the way is better than standing still. I was not afraid of the twin bogeys of Revisionism and Reformism. We needed to revise and reform a bit in the Party and to stop worrying about right deviations and left phrasemongering.

I agitated. "We must join other organizations. Let us take night courses. Let's join the C.C.F. Let's make friends with everyone, even conservatives."

My agitation was not received very well in the Party. Agitation and proposals of change from the lower units were not welcome, were, somehow, viewed with suspicion. Who knows what I would be accused of! (Jim Davis, much to his bewilderment, was charged with "anarcho-syndicalism" when his trade union activities were found not entirely satisfactory to some higher cadres.)

I was reproved by a member of the City Committee who made a speech at our unit meeting. I was accused of bringing in reformism, wanting to dilute our program and aims, and of hobnobbing with questionable elements.

"If you have other ideas for the Party, wait until the next Convention and present them there," he advised. "As for me, I could not be friends with a Conservative, nor do I think we should be."

But I was already friends with a Conservative — indeed, with a Baptist too—and I could not wait until the next Convention. Besides, I recalled what had happened to Harry Fistell and I decided to act now.

"Indeed, I think I can be friends with a Conservative," I answered and, not waiting until the end of the meeting, I walked out.

Nor was I worried about what I left behind, for I knew instinctively that for such as me there would be no lack of greener pastures.

*In 1963 I was recruited into the N.D.P. by a neighbor, Alderman Horace Brown. We did some fine work in the ensuing Federal elections in the Spadina Riding.

www.ingramcontent.com/pod-product-compliance
Lightning Source LLC
Chambersburg PA
CBHW050800160426
43192CB00010B/1589